C000299367

Questions God Asks

Tony Bennett

DayOne

Endorsements

What perhaps is needed more than ever in our day is for Christians to be meaningfully engaging with the Bible every day. In this devotional book which looks at thirty-one questions asked either by God in the Old Testament or by Jesus in the New Testament, Tony Bennett helps us to do just that. He both clearly and helpfully explains the text in its setting and also prompts the reader to respond with reflective points aimed to engage the heart and mind. As I read these chapters, I felt my heart warmed as my gaze was directed toward God and His Son, Jesus Christ. I also found myself deeply challenged. This will help Christians get into the Word and be fed by it. I highly recommend this thirty-one-day devotional and will certainly be commending it to our church congregation.

Chris Durrant, Pastor, Howeth Road Evangelical Church, Bournemouth

Tony Bennett has added another wonderful volume to his Day One series of daily devotional studies. Packed, pithy, and pointing us to Christ, he guides us with wisdom and clarity, shedding fresh light on well-known texts as well as unearthing less common treasures. Apposite illustrations punctuate the text and applicatory questions invite us deeper. Accessible to all, I will be commending this to my congregation, while I expect many a preacher will glean here, as I have done, the seeds of a sermon, the outline of a series, and a fund of stories.

Andy Saville, Vicar, All Saints, Laleham

First published in Great Britain in 2021 by
DayOne, Ryelands Road, Leominster, HR6 8NZ
Email: sales@dayone.co.uk
Website: www.dayone.co.uk

British Library Cataloguing in Publication Data
A record for this book is available from the British Library

ISBN: 978 1 84625 685 1

Cover design by Kathryn Chedgzoy

Printed by 4Edge

To my
Bible Study companions
Gordon, Nick, Charlie and Andy.

Contents

Preface

This is now my fourth volume of short expositions intended to provide one month's daily reflections on a biblical theme. The first two volumes each took thirty-one verses of Scripture containing the phrase 'But God'—or 'But Jesus' in the New Testament; the third reflected on thirty-one verses containing the phrase 'But Now'. The first chapter in the first volume was entitled 'God's First Question' in which we considered God's first recorded question to Adam. Adam and his wife, tempted by the devil, had disobeyed God's clear command not to eat from the tree of the knowledge of good and evil and were now trying to hide themselves from God in the garden. Scripture records:

> And they heard the sound of the Lord God walking in the garden in the cool of the day, and the man and his wife hid themselves from the presence of the Lord God among the trees of the garden. But the Lord God called to the man and said to him, 'Where are you?' (Gen. 3:8–9).

Now this raises the interesting thought in our minds as to why the all-knowing God would ask a question at all. After all, we ask questions to seek information—to discover something we don't know. In that first chapter, I pointed out that the Bible records God—and Jesus—

asking numerous questions of people, such as Cain (Gen. 4:9), Elijah (1 Kings 19:9) and Peter (John 21:15–17) to name but three. I quoted Peter Williams as saying that God's questions 'are meant to teach us something, or to expose to us our inner selves when we are guilty of sin or disobedience'.[1] So whenever we come across God asking a question, our response should be, 'Is God addressing that question to me, and if so what am I meant to learn from it?'

This volume picks up where that first chapter left off by looking at thirty-one questions recorded in the Bible that were asked either by God in the Old Testament or by Jesus in the New Testament. In the Old Testament, I have chosen mostly questions that God asked to named individuals—Cain, Abraham, Moses, Elijah, Isaiah, Jeremiah and Ezekiel—but some were posed through God's prophets to his people in general. Again, in the New Testament, although some of Jesus' questions are asked rhetorically during his public preaching, many are posed to specific people such as Simon the Pharisee, Nicodemus, Martha, Philip, the Emmaus Road disciples and Peter.

To most of these questions, Scripture records no answer. Cain answers God's question to him with a lie (Gen. 3:9)! Simon the Pharisee (Luke 7:43) and an unnamed lawyer (Luke 10:37) answer honestly, but somewhat grudgingly giving the underlying sense of, 'Well, okay I suppose you're right.' But this raises the interesting question of,

'How should we answer the questions in our own hearts as we read these verses?' And as well as examples to avoid, you will find some examples to follow—Ezekiel (Ezek. 37:3), Martha (John 11:27) and Peter (John 6:68; 21:15–17) come to mind. But maybe the reason why God doesn't give us all the answers to his questions in Scripture is because he wants us, through the teaching of his Holy Spirit, to be offering our own answers so that we might honestly search our own hearts and see in them what he already sees and knows. So may we read these expositions prayerfully, having in our hearts this prayer of the psalmist:

> Search me, O God, and know my heart!
> Try me and know my thoughts!
> And see if there be any grievous way in me,
> and lead me in the way everlasting.
>
> (Psalm 139:23–24)

Tony Bennett
Lymington, Hampshire
May 2021

When God asks
the questions

Chapter 1

Why are you angry, and why has your face fallen? ...
Where is Abel your brother?

Genesis 4:6, 9

G od's first recorded question was asked of Adam—
'Where are you?' (Gen. 3:9)—after he and Eve had
disobeyed God's clear command to not eat the fruit of the
tree in the midst of the Garden of Eden. Just over twenty
verses later, we have God's second question. And three
verses after that, we have the third. Now the all-knowing
God never asks a question because he lacks knowledge. So
whenever we come across a God-asked question in the Bible
our response should be, 'Is God addressing that question to
me, and, if so, what am I meant to learn from it?'

But first, we need to establish the context of this
exchange between God and Cain. At the end of Genesis
3, God drove Adam and Eve from the garden, placing an
angelic guard against their return. Chapter 4 opens with
the first two human births—Eve giving birth first to Cain
who becomes 'a worker of the ground', and then Abel who
'was a keeper of sheep'. And so we read: 'In the course
of time Cain brought to the LORD an offering of the fruit
of the ground, and Abel also brought of the firstborn of
his flock and of their fat portions' (vv. 3–4). Given their
occupations there is nothing very surprising in that, but
then we read: 'And the LORD had regard for Abel and his

offering, but for Cain and his offering he had no regard' (vv. 4–5).

And at that point we all ask the same question: 'Why did God accept one offering and not the other?' But if we read the text carefully, we might see that that is not the right question to ask, or at least not before we've asked another question. Let me explain. If you look carefully at verses 4–5, you'll see that the focus of God's response—his acceptance of one and his rejection of the other—is not first and foremost the offerings, but the people who brought them: 'And the LORD had regard for Abel and his offering, but for Cain and his offering he had no regard.' So the question we need to ask first must focus on the givers, not the gifts.

In Hebrews 11:4 we read that 'by faith Abel offered to God a more acceptable sacrifice than Cain.' So the best explanation is 'the heart condition of the one bringing the offering'.[1] Abel came in faith; Cain came in arrogance. The former is testified by Scripture; the latter is evidenced by the unfolding drama.

And that leads us to the second Scripture that reveals why God only accepted Abel and his offering. For it wasn't that the two brothers brought the same offering, one that was received because of faith while the other was rejected for unbelief. The offerings were different, 'and in that difference we see the faith of one and the unbelief of the other'.[2] God had already shown to Cain and Abel's parents what kind of sacrifice was required for a sin-offering. After

Adam and Eve had sinned in the Garden, we are told that 'the LORD God made for Adam and for his wife garments of skin and clothed them' (Gen. 3:21). In other words, God had dealt with their sin by slaying an innocent animal—a spotless substitute—which pointed forward to the Passover, the whole sacrificial system of the tabernacle and the temple, and most significantly to the substitutionary death of Christ at Calvary. That is why Abel's offering 'of the firstborn of the flock and of their fat portions'—of only the very best—was acceptable to God. He offered what was acceptable to God, not merely what was convenient to him.

So what lessons does this teach us? First, that you can be accepted by God only by faith, and only through the blood of the sacrifice that God has provided. You cannot come to God any way you choose. As one Bible commentator explains:

> That is the problem with so many 'religious people.' They come to God with their beautiful offerings. But God rejects them and their godless worship. There is no blood, no Christ and hence no true Christianity, however beautiful their service might be.[3]

In verse 5, we discover Cain's response: he was 'very angry and his face fell'. But note the mercy of God in verse 6 where we read that 'the LORD said to Cain, "Why are you angry, and why has your face fallen?"' And this in Scripture is God's second question. And here God strives with Cain—as he mercifully does with us—to divert him from sin. God, as it were, preaches Cain his own sermon warning him that 'sin is crouching at the door'. But Cain is deaf to the wise counsels of God.

In the very next verse, Cain kills his brother Abel. This confirms what Cain's heart must have been like when he brought his offering. You don't go straight from godly living to killing your brother in four verses! Cain had doubtless hoped that by bringing his offering to God 'he could cover up his unrepentantly evil life with an air of respectability'.[4] But God saw through his hypocrisy—and sadly he will see through yours and mine. Which brings us to God's third question: 'Then the LORD said to Cain, "Where is Abel your brother?"' (v. 9). Cain's answer is Scripture's first recorded lie—'I do not know'—followed by Scripture's first recorded human question, 'Am I my brother's keeper?' This is even worse than the lie. What arrogance does this show in the heart of man—the same arrogance as when we deny our sinfulness and question God's perfect justice. And yet it also shows God's grace in that he never wants us to remain in our sin, and will pursue us when we do sin—'whether it's Adam in the garden, Cain outside the garden, the woman of Samaria at the well, or the one lost sheep, he is always pursuing us'.[5]

So as we hear these two divinely-asked questions, it is good to search our own hearts. Do we come to God in the way we desire or the way he commands? Do we seek to make our own amends for our sin or do we trust only in the provision that God has made for the forgiveness of sin—through the blood of his only begotten Son? Are you attentive to God's voice when, through his Word, he poses those searching questions that he wants to be the means to bring you to—or back to—himself?

> Search our hearts, we pray, Lord; shine your light within,
> When we call our failings anything but sin.
> Proud of our achievements, though our aims are wrong;
> You can see our motives, tainted all along.
> You, O Christ, can cleanse us, judge us and forgive:
> In the light you give us let us walk, and live.[6]

FOR FURTHER READING: GENESIS 4:1–16

Reflect on these points:

1. *Whenever we come across a God-asked question in the Bible our response should be, 'Is God addressing that question to me, and, if so, what am I meant to learn from it?' Abel offered what was acceptable to God, not merely what was convenient to him.*

2. *Are you attentive to God's voice when through his Word he poses those searching questions that he wants to be the means to bring you to—or back to—himself?*

Our God
is faithful

Chapter 2

Is anything too hard for the Lord?

Genesis 18:14

Picture the scene. It's a typical, stiflingly-hot early afternoon in the desert. As always at about this time, life has slowed down—if not stopped. The ninety-nine-year-old patriarch is sitting in the entrance to his tent with the side flaps open, desperately trying to catch the tiniest bit of desert breeze. It's a scene of calm and gentle snoozing. But then, in a trice, everything changes. Seemingly from nowhere, three men appear and stand in front of Abraham. The pace of life suddenly accelerates. Just look at the words: Abraham hurried (Gen. 18:2), and hurried again (v. 6), 'quick' he tells Sarah in the same verse, before running (v. 7) and the servants hurried! And not every wife would appreciate being addressed as Sarah is by her husband in verse 6. Literally: 'Quick! Three seahs of fine flour! Knead it and make loaves!' No 'please' or 'thank you' there!

What brings about this sudden burst of early-afternoon activity? Nothing more than Abraham's desire to offer the best hospitality to complete strangers. And although the inspired writer lets us in on the secret about these three, it's very clear from Scripture that, at the time, Abraham doesn't know who they are. We're told right at the start (v. 1) that one of them is 'the Lord': 'The Lord appeared to Abraham near the great trees of Mamre.' God himself,

21

of course, is invisible spirit and as Christopher Wright reminds us, 'he cannot be seen in a physical sense in his essence as God'.[1] But God did make human beings in his own image and it was perfectly natural for God to take human form when he wanted to engage in conversation in such a direct way as here with Abraham.

By verse 9 the sumptuous meal is over and it's time for the after-dinner conversation, and there are two topics. The main part of the conversation will concern the fate of Sodom and Gomorrah. But first, God confirms his promise of a son for Abraham and Sarah—an idea that strikes the eaves-dropping Sarah as preposterously comic. Yet here, as in the story of Cain and Abel, we see the all-seeing eye and all-hearing ear of God. For although Scripture tells us that Sarah was inside the tent, 'listening at the tent door' (v. 10) and therefore out of human eyesight, and that she 'laughed to herself' (v. 12), the Lord immediately asks Abraham, 'Why did Sarah laugh and say, "Shall I indeed bear a child, now that I am old?"' (v. 13). How humbling to realise all that God sees and all that God hears as we go about our daily lives! And then the Lord adds one of the most wonderful questions asked by God recorded in the Bible. 'Is anything too hard for the LORD?' (v. 14).[2]

Now first, let me be clear: from this question we are not meant to learn that God will do anything incredible for us if we simply exercise enough positive thinking. But we can—indeed we should—apply this verse with the same meaning it has in the original text: namely that God will do what he has promised, even though it seems incredible. The question is tied to a promise and we must use it that way. And God does make incredible promises to us—of forgiveness of sin (Eph. 1:7) and of our eternal security with him (John 10:28), to name but two.

What God is asking of Abraham and Sarah in Genesis 18 is whether they think there is any circumstance in their life that he cannot control. And notice how God directs them—and us—away from the perceived problem to himself. The equivalent passage in the New Testament is Jesus' encounter with a man whose son had been afflicted by an unclean spirit from his childhood. The boy's father says to Jesus: 'And it has often cast him into the fire and into the water, to destroy him. But if you can do anything, have compassion on us and help us.' Jesus replies: 'If you can! All things are possible for the one who believes' (Mark 9:22–23). Both this man and Sarah exhibited unbelief in the power of God. And as John Stott writes: 'Unbelief is not a misfortune to be pitied; it is a sin to be deplored. Its sinfulness lies in the fact that it contradicts the Word of the one true God and thus attributes falsehoods to him.'[3]

The New Testament helps us to see some of the truly wonderful things that God is able to do for those who turn to him in repentance and faith. We have a God who is, 'able to save to the uttermost those who draw near to God' (Heb. 7:25); 'able to help those who are being tempted' (Heb. 2:18); and 'able to make all grace abound to you' (2 Cor. 9:8).

Back in Genesis 18, where Sarah, confronted with her disbelieving laugh at God's promise to Abraham, denies everything. 'I did not laugh', she claims—Scripture adding, 'for she was afraid' (v. 15). If she hadn't up to this point realised who this visitor was, then she certainly had now, for who other than God could hear her 'laugh to herself' and detect words inaudible to the human ear? No wonder she was afraid!

The story ends surprisingly abruptly. 'No, but you did laugh,' replies the Lord and the subject is dropped, never to be mentioned again. But there are three postscripts that mustn't go unnoticed. First, God keeps this remarkable promise. And three chapters further on, we read these wonderful words: 'The LORD visited Sarah as he had said, and the LORD did to Sarah as he had promised. And Sarah conceived and bore Abraham a son in his old age at the time of which God had spoken to him' (Gen. 21:1–2). God never fails, and God is never late. He always keeps to his timetable. One Bible commentator writes: 'God is a God of his word. If he were not, the universe would fall apart.'[4] Second, we mustn't miss the significance of the name given by Abraham and Sarah to their newborn son. They name him Isaac, which means 'he laughs'! And Sarah adds: 'God has made laughter for me; everyone who hears will laugh over me' (Gen. 21:6). And third, we have it on biblical authority that Sarah learnt from her experience. Her gracious and forgiving God even had her included in the roll-call of the faithful in Hebrews 11 where we read: 'By faith Sarah herself received power to conceive, even when she was past the age, since she considered him faithful who had promised' (Heb. 11:11). Sarah had come to learn that the answer to God's question was, 'No—nothing is too hard for the Lord!' Are you, like Sarah, 'fully convinced that God [is] able to do what he has promised' (Rom. 4:21)?

> From the breaking of the dawn to the setting of
>   the sun,
> I will stand on every promise of Your Word,
> Words of power, strong to save, that will never
>   pass away;
> I will stand on every promise of Your Word.
> For your covenant is sure, and on this I am secure;
> I can stand on every promise of Your Word.[5]

FOR FURTHER READING: GENESIS 18:1–15

Reflect on these points:

1. *What are we meant to learn from God's question to Abraham, 'Is anything too hard for the Lord?'*

2. *'Unbelief is not a misfortune to be pitied; it is a sin to be deplored' (John Stott).*

3. *God never fails, and God is never late. He always keeps to his timetable.*

The excuse factory

Chapter 3

Who has made man's mouth?

Exodus 4:11

Surrey police recently published some of the excuses their officers have been given when stopping motorists who were using a mobile phone whilst driving. 'It was my ex-wife harassing me. Can you speak to her?' 'I was just telling them I couldn't answer as I was driving.' 'I wasn't calling anyone, I was replying to an e-mail.' But we are all inveterate excuse factories, forever trying to suggest that what we did, or what we want to do is right even when we know that is not the case. And in the fourth chapter of Exodus, Moses is caught in excuse-making mode. But first some context.

Joseph is dead and 'there arose a new king in Egypt who did not know Joseph' (Ex. 1:8). The new Pharaoh oppresses the Israelites with harsh labour, even ordering the Egyptian midwives to kill their new-born males. As a result of an extraordinary turn of events (Ex. 2:1–10), Moses—the son of an Israelite couple—is adopted by Pharaoh's daughter and ends up as a young adult in Pharaoh's court. But having killed an Egyptian whom he saw beating an Israelite, Moses flees to Midian where he later marries Zipporah, a daughter of a Midianite priest (Ex. 2:11–21). Moses is enjoying the life of a happily-married shepherd in Midian but God has other plans and trouble comes when God's plans clash with Moses' wishes.

How often we find ourselves in the same position—with God's will and plan for our lives clearly pointing in one direction, whilst our own desire is to take a different path. 'God wants me as a single person at least for the moment, but I want to be married—now.' 'God wants me to be more fully involved in the life of his church, but I want to concentrate on my career and earn more money.' And your response? To obey, or, like Moses, to offer excuses?

In Exodus 3, God appears to Moses in the midst of a burning bush—fire being an image of God's holiness—and commissions him to return to Egypt and lead God's rescue of the enslaved Israelites. Let the excuse-making begin! First, Moses says he's a nobody. No one knows who he is, and he gives voice to his sense of personal inadequacy. 'But I will be with you,' replies God (v. 12). When God commissions us, we don't need to be 'adequate' because God always equips us for the tasks he gives us. With his first excuse floored, Moses tries again. If the first excuse was, 'Nobody knows who I am,' now the second excuse was, 'Nobody knows who you are!' Says Moses to God: 'If I come to the people of Israel and say to them, "The God of your fathers has sent me to you," and they ask me, "What is his name?" what shall I say to them?' (v. 13). And God replies: 'I am who I am'—an answer which Alec Motyer describes as 'endlessly satisfying and bafflingly enigmatic',[1] and it shows us the 'ever-present, ever-active, interventionist-for-good, ever-independent, sovereign God'.[2]

You might have thought that would close out the conversation. But no! In chapter 4, Moses presses on with excuse number three, 'they won't believe me' (v. 1), and excuse number four (v. 10), 'Oh, my LORD, I am not eloquent, either in the past or since you have spoken to your servant, but I am slow of speech and of tongue.' It's not entirely clear what it is that Moses is referring to in saying this. Did he lack confidence as a public speaker. Or did he, like Britain's King George VI, have a stammer? Whatever it was, one commentator rightly points out that what Moses had 'was not so much a speech problem as an obedience problem'.[3] But Moses was not only disobedient, he was also mistaken. For he seemed to think that 'the gift of oratory is a prime pre-requisite for effective ministry'.[4] And how often do we make the same mistake today?

It's clear that Moses is thinking too much about himself. 'Who am I that I should go?' (3:11), 'What shall I say?' (3:13), 'They will not believe me or listen to my voice' (4:1), 'I am not eloquent ... but I am slow of speech' (4:10). And in his tender and gracious reply, God turns Moses eyes from himself to his God. The irony is that Moses has been calling God 'LORD'—a word that means sovereign or master. As Alec Motyer comments: 'In a way it is both sad and understandable that Moses appeals to the Sovereign One—a title implying "You can do anything and everything you wish"—but goes on to make his own inabilities the determinative factor.' Motyer adds: 'This is a theological version of having your cake and eating it if ever there was one!'[5] Yes, God will take our feelings of inadequacy seriously, but he will still tell us to act on the basis of the God we profess to believe in. In the New Testament era, he will come to us in our fears and say:

> Turn your eyes upon Jesus,
> Look full in his wonderful face;
> And the things of earth will grow strangely dim
> In the light of his glory and grace.[6]

And God says to Moses—and he says to you and to me—'Don't refuse to go because of what you are, but go because of what I am!'[7]

God's answer to Moses, in the form of three rhetorical questions, cut right through Moses' argument. 'Who has made man's mouth? Who makes him mute, or deaf, or seeing, or blind? Is it not I, the LORD?' (v. 11). As David reminds us in the Psalms, each of us is 'fearfully and wonderfully made' (Ps. 139:14), and God will use us just as he created us. And to Moses, God gives this further assurance: 'Now therefore go, and I will be with your mouth and teach you what you shall speak' (v. 12).

Sadly, Moses still won't either believe or go. 'Oh, my LORD, please send someone else,' he bleats in verse 13. Again, God is patient with his servant and provides his brother Aaron to accompany him on the mission. But that concession by God would bring its own challenges for Moses. After all, it was Aaron who would make the golden calf (Exodus 32) and Aaron—along with his sister Miriam—who was critical of Moses and his Midianite wife thereby bringing trouble on the Hebrew camp (Numbers 12).

Right at the end of the biblical account of Moses' life, we find out that God knew Moses better than he knew himself, for we find Moses delivering his farewell sermon to the Israelites—a little matter of 123 verses (Deut. 29:2–32:47)! Not bad for someone who was 'not eloquent' and 'slow of speech and of tongue'. So when we're faced with the daunting prospect of obeying God's will for our lives, another hymn writer comes with godly advice:

> Can we find a friend so faithful,
> Who will all our sorrows share?
> Jesus knows our every weakness—
> Take it to the Lord in prayer![8]

FOR FURTHER READING: EXODUS 3:1–4:17

Reflect on these points:

1. *What do we do when we find ourselves in the position of God's will and plan for our lives clearly pointing in one direction, whilst our own desire is to take a different path?*

2. *God will take our feelings of inadequacy seriously, but he will still tell us to act on the basis of the God we profess to believe in.*

God's broken-hearted servant

Chapter 4

What are you doing here, Elijah?

1 Kings 19:9

Elizabeth Clephane was born on 18 June 1830, in West Circus Place, Edinburgh. The grand terrace of Georgian houses still stands today looking like Edinburgh's answer to Bath's Royal Crescent. She was the third daughter of the county sheriff of Fife, Andrew Clephane, and his wife Anna. Much of her short life was spent forty miles south-east of Edinburgh in the small town of Melrose on the Scottish borders where the townsfolk referred to her affectionately as 'the Sunbeam' because of her acts of Christian kindness towards the poor of the town. Afflicted with ill health for much of her short life—she died aged just thirty-eight—she would be best remembered for the hymns she wrote, published after her death under the title 'Breathings on the Border'. That title possibly had a spiritual as well as a geographic meaning. Her most famous hymn, 'Beneath the Cross of Jesus', was written just before she died.[1] In that hymn, she wrote how that:

> From my stricken heart, with tears,
>
> Two wonders I confess,
>
> The wonders of redeeming love,
>
> And my own worthlessness.

These are sentiments that may echo in your own experience, and they have something in common with the prophet Elijah when we find him alone on Mount Horeb in 1 Kings 19.

Elijah has just confronted Ahab and the prophets of Baal in which God wins a famous victory and Elijah then orders the killing of the evil prophets. Maybe Elijah had presumed that after such spectacular displays of God's sovereign power that the king, his queen and the people would wholeheartedly turn back to God. But nothing of the sort happened. Indeed, quite the reverse, and Queen Jezebel sends a message to Elijah which says, 'So may the gods do to me and more also, if I do not make your life as the life of one of [those prophets of Baal] by this time tomorrow' (v. 2). In most modern translations we then read that Elijah 'was afraid' and ran for his life first to Beersheba (v. 3) and then to Mount Horeb (v. 8). But a number offer a footnote that Elijah 'saw' and ran for his life. Indeed, the New King James Version reads: 'And when he saw that'—in other words when he saw Jezebel's threatening message—'he arose and ran for his life'.[2] And how we read verse 3 will colour the meaning of what follows and God's famous question, 'What are you doing here, Elijah?' (v. 9). To put this in common language: is Elijah a man or a mouse? And therefore does God's question have overtones of compassion or of criticism?

If, indeed, it was fear that made Elijah run from Jezebel then we certainly should feel for him. Most of us shrivel up at the first sign or sound of opposition to the gospel or to biblical faith—let alone a genuine death threat. And if God knew that Elijah was acting like a spiritual mouse, just look at how gracious he was to him. Midway through Elijah's journey as he slept under a tree, God provides him 'at his head' with 'a cake baked on hot stones and a jar of water' (v. 6). As Philip Ryken comments: 'How is this for room service!'[3] And when we're fearful, God always comes to those who are truly his servants and holds us fast.

And sometimes God will, in his grace, come to us in a place where in our heart of hearts we know that we should not be, and enquire, 'What are you doing here?' Listen to that voice, answer honestly to the one who knows the secrets of your heart, and be obedient to it. And just as God re-commissions Elijah (vv. 15–18), so he will do to you.

But, as we've already hinted, there is biblical evidence to suggest that might not have been Elijah's position. Maybe he believed that true repentance would now come to Israel and the failure of the king and the queen—and the nation— to turn back to God breaks his heart. In this reading of the text, Elijah is not terrified by Jezebel but broken-hearted by her unrepentant paganism. This is not self-pity but being rightly jealous of God's reputation. Dale Ralph Davis suggests other textual reasons to follow this line of interpretation: God's repeated ministering to Elijah during his journey (vv. 5–8); God's reference to 'the journey' that is 'too great for you' suggesting this is a God-approved mission, not a Jonah-like manoeuvre; Elijah's coming to Horeb—'the mount of God' (v. 8)—where he had appeared to Moses in the burning bush, brought water out of the rock, delivered the Ten Commandments and hid Moses in the cleft of the rock whilst his glory passed by. This really is God's place. This is not Tarshish! And thus, Davis suggests that God's question—'What are you doing here, Elijah?'—is meant in the sense of: 'What are you doing here, Elijah, at Moses' Place, at the Covenant Connection, Elijah, where I myself [v. 7] have led you to come?'[4]

Read thus, God's question is not so much a correction as an invitation—an invitation to a broken-hearted servant to pour out your burdened heart to the Lord. And what does God promise to the broken-hearted? 'The LORD is near to the broken-hearted and saves the crushed in spirit' (Ps. 34:18). And again, 'He heals the broken-hearted and binds up their wounds' (Ps. 147:3). And the passage from Isaiah that our Lord reads in the synagogue at Nazareth includes the words that 'he has sent me to bind up the broken-hearted...' (Is. 61:1).

And Jesus tells the Nazareth congregation—and he tells us—'Today this Scripture has been fulfilled in your hearing' (Luke 4:21).

That's why, as wonderful as it is to read, we don't need to see and hear what Elijah saw and heard—the wind, the earthquake, the fire, and 'the still, small voice' (1 Kings 19:12, KJV). For the God of that still, small voice is shown to us in the pages of Scripture: in the birth of his Son, his healing ministry, his grieving with the bereaved, his forgiveness of penitent sinners, his donkey ride into Jerusalem in kingly humility, but most supremely in his sacrificial and atoning death at Calvary. And that brings us full circle as we reflect—in our broken-heartedness—upon the truth that:

> Upon that cross of Jesus
> Mine eye at times can see
> The very dying form of One
> Who suffered there for me:
> And from my stricken heart with tears
> Two wonders I confess,
> The wonders of redeeming love
> And my own worthlessness.[5]

FOR FURTHER READING: 1 KINGS 19:1–18

Reflect on these points:

1. *When we're fearful, God always comes to those who are truly his servants and holds us fast.*

2. *Sometimes God will, in his grace, come to us in a place where in our heart of hearts we know that we should not be, and enquire, 'What are you doing here?'*

Holy, Holy, Holy!

Chapter 5

Whom shall I send, and who will go for us?

Isaiah 6:8

A s I write this chapter, Britain is embroiled in Brexit. We certainly live in a time of great national upheaval and uncertainty. Maybe we fear that the country has lost its bearings—political, economic, moral and spiritual. The comedian David Schneider recently commented: 'I'm increasingly convinced that God has taken a sabbatical ... and has left a hopelessly unqualified intern in charge!'[1] And in this sense, Isaiah is very much a prophet for our times. For he was speaking to a nation where religious leaders were trapped in a vacuum of theological and moral uncertainty, and where political leaders had lost their bearings.

In Isaiah 5, God had delivered a devastating exposure of corruption, greed, religious formalism, hypocrisy and cynicism towards himself. Then verse 1 of Isaiah chapter 6 clearly anchors the events in 740 BC—the year that King Uzziah died. The first four decades of his fifty-two-year reign were years of peace and prosperity for Judah as the king 'did what was right in the eyes of the LORD' (2 Chr. 26:4), but then he went into the temple to burn incense in clear contravention of God's law, and God struck him and he ended his life as a leper. Uzziah started well but finished badly. And now God is saying, 'Just remember Uzziah.' He's, as it were, a parable of the nation's pride and disobedience. But the future isn't as grim as the end of chapter 5 suggests, because our God is a God of grace, and there's always more grace. And as we consider this chapter's first eight verses, we see three things: the holiness of God (vv. 1–4); the sinfulness of mankind (v. 5); and the graciousness of God (vv. 6–8).

As chapter 6 opens Isaiah is transported, as it were, to the throne room of heaven where he sees 'the LORD' (v. 1). Uzziah may be dead, but this King is alive. He is 'from everlasting to everlasting' (Ps. 90:2). National governments may be something of an omni-shambles, but there's no crisis in heaven where God is on the throne 'high and lifted up'. Indeed, God himself is so indescribable, that Isaiah settles for giving us descriptions of the throne and mere hem of the King's robe. Now the Duchess of Cambridge had a train to her wedding dress that was nine feet long—but there was still room for a number of other people to get into Westminster Abbey! But God's robe, Isaiah tells us, filled the temple! And if the hem fills the temple, then how great is that robe? And how great is that throne? And how great is that Divine Being? Indeed, 'the whole earth is full of his glory!' (v. 3). What's more, we learn from the angelic chorus that God is not just holy, but 'holy, holy, holy', and this is not mere repetition, it's emphasis. John Mackay tells us that this 'divine holiness is the unsullied and immaculate ethical purity of the God who is absolutely opposed to sin and evil in all its manifestations'.[2]

That's why when we see even a glimpse of the holiness of God we become acutely aware of our own sinfulness. As Thomas Binney (1798–1874) asked:

> O how shall I, whose native sphere
> Is dark, whose mind is dim,
> Before the Ineffable appear,
> And on my naked spirit bear
> The uncreated beam?[3]

'Woe is me! For I am lost,' exclaims Isaiah—or as J.B. Phillips has it, 'I'm finished!'—'for I am a man of unclean lips, and I dwell in the midst of a people of unclean lips; for my eyes have seen the King, the LORD of hosts!' (v. 5). Have you come to that point, when you suddenly realise that against God's utter holiness, degrees of sin become irrelevant. It's the only appropriate response. It was Peter's response: 'Depart from me, for I am a sinful man, O LORD' (Luke 5:8). It was the prodigal son's response: 'Father, I have sinned against heaven and before you. I am no longer worthy to be called your son' (Luke 15:18–19). It was the tax collector's response in Jesus' parable: 'God, be merciful to me, a sinner!' (Luke 18:13). Has it been your response?

But then we see that there's nothing Isaiah—or we—can do about this problem. Only God can solve the problem of sin. One of the seraphim—throne room attendants of God who first appeared in verse 2—then brings a burning coal from the altar (v. 6), and puts it on Isaiah's lips, pronouncing: 'Behold, this has touched your lips; your guilt is taken away, and your sin atoned for' (v. 7). This must have been utterly frightening, but this is not God coming in judgement, but in grace and mercy. We have here the symbolism of the provision God had made for the atonement for sin through each Israelite's burnt offering which 'shall be accepted for him to make atonement for him' (Lev. 1:4). David Turner describes these verses in Isaiah 6 as 'Amazing Grace, Old Testament style', adding that 'God gives what God demands—a holy sacrifice for sin'.[4] It is, in the title of John Murray's Christian classic, Redemption Accomplished and Applied.[5] And it's only when we see our sin as God sees it that we will see our need of that atoning sacrifice. But God has graciously provided it in Jesus who gives himself on the altar—the Cross at Calvary—because it is 'the blood of Jesus his Son [that] cleanses us from all sin' (1 John 1:7). The next verse of Binney's hymn tells us:

> There is a way for man to rise
> To that sublime abode:
> An offering and a sacrifice,
> A Holy Spirit's energies,
> An Advocate with God.

And it's only when Isaiah has been cleansed that he can be commissioned. It's the same for us—which leads us to God's question. You might have thought that the effect of this wondrous vision on Isaiah would be some great emotional high, but no, the result is that he now wants to be a servant of the God who has so graciously and freely redeemed him. 'And I heard the voice of the LORD saying, "Who shall I send, and who will go for us?" Then I said, "Here I am! Send me"' (v. 8).

Conviction, confession, cleansing and commissioning. It has to be in that order. And for us it has to be only through Christ. What God does for Isaiah, he can do for you and for me for when he intervenes, 'sinful rebels are turned into loving servants'.[6] God is still the same holy, glorious, reigning and gracious King he was in the year that King Uzziah died. And when all the heads of states of every nation upon this earth have died, God will still be King:

> So be it Lord, Your throne shall never
> Like earth's proud empires, pass away;
> Your kingdom stands and grows for ever,
> Till all Your creatures own Your sway.[7]

FOR FURTHER READING: ISAIAH 6:1–8

Reflect on these points:

1. *'Divine holiness is the unsullied and immaculate ethical purity of the God who is absolutely opposed to sin and evil in all its manifestations' (John Mackay).*

2. *It's only when we see our sin as God sees it that we will see our need of that atoning sacrifice.*

How Great
Thou Art!

Chapter 6

*To whom then will you compare me, that I should be
like him?*

Isaiah 40:25

Isaiah is a long book. Its sixty-six chapters outnumber
all the other books of the Bible—except the 150 psalms.
And in terms of verses, its 1,292 are beaten by only
Genesis and Jeremiah. Isaiah is also very much a book of
two halves: chapters 1–39 and 40–66. During the first
half, God is addressing the sins of his people—notably
greed, idolatry and a lack of social justice. But there are
also clear hints of God's promised Messiah: 'The virgin
shall conceive and bear a son, and shall call his name
Immanuel' (7:14); 'For to us a child is born, to us a son
is given' (9:6); 'There shall come forth a shoot from the
stump of Jesse' (11:1). In chapter 39, Isaiah prophesied
that Judah would go into exile in Babylon (v. 6) and just
over a century later they did. So from chapter 40, Isaiah
is no longer addressing the people of his own day. By the
Holy Spirit, he is being projected into the future and is
preaching the gospel to Jews languishing in Babylonian
exile. He tells them: 'God has not abandoned you. He still
has a gracious purpose for you, and he will come and save
you.' And as we read these chapters, we are also meant to
see that Isaiah is not just speaking about God's rescue of
Israel from exile in Babylon, but also our rescue from the
slavery of sin. George Frideric Handel (1685–1759) was

spot on when he included extracts from Isaiah 40 in his oratorio Messiah.

So in the first eleven verses of Isaiah 40, we have prophecies of John the Baptist (v. 3), Christ's incarnation (v. 5), and the Good Shepherd (v. 11)—and these verses are quoted in the New Testament.[1] William Philip sees these verses as 'the prophecy of the four voices': the voice of the prophets speaking comfort (vv. 1–2); the voice of deliverance from bondage (vv. 3–5); the voice of the power of God's Word (vv. 6–8); and the voice of both the power and gentleness of God (vv. 9–11).[2]

So here is Isaiah presenting us with the outline of the Christian gospel. So why don't we immediately believe it? Because, says Isaiah, we don't have a biblical view of God. In his sermons on this chapter, Martyn Lloyd-Jones asks:

> How often have you heard sermons about God? We are all interested in what we want and need. We start with ourselves—we are introspective and self-centred. Our thoughts revolve around ourselves. We think we are the centre of the universe. But we are not, my friends. So here in verses 12–17, Isaiah brings us face to face with God.[3]

And in these verses, we read of four aspects of God's being and character: his greatness and power (v. 12); his wisdom (vv. 13–14); and his transcendent glory (v. 16). Furthermore, Isaiah wants us to see is that we are the polar opposite of God, for we are insignificant (vv. 15, 17), foolish (vv. 19–20) and unfailingly ordinary (vv. 22, 24). The comparison is stated thus:

> Do you not know? Do you not hear?
> Has it not been told you from the beginning?
> Have you not understood from the
> foundations of the earth?
> It is he who sits above the circle of the earth,
> and its inhabitants are like grasshoppers.
>
> (vv. 21–22)

Even the world leaders are under God's jurisdiction (v. 23) as Isaiah's contemporaries had recently witnessed. In comparison to God, we're like stubble that the wind blows away (v. 24). So as you look back over history—over Sennacherib, Nebuchadnezzar, Alexander, Napoleon, Hitler, Stalin, Mao, and add our present day world leaders to the list—are you not wanting to sing with the hymn writer of old:

> Frail as summer's flower we flourish;
> Blows the wind, and it is gone.
> But while mortals rise and perish,
> God endures unchanging on.
> Praise Him! Praise Him!
> Praise the high eternal One.[4]

Once we have a right view of God, we are ready to hear God's question in verse 25. Indeed, it's the same question Isaiah posed in verse 18, but this time it's spoken by God.

'"To whom then will you compare me, that I should be like him?" says the Holy One.' Like many of God's question, the answer is obvious: 'No one!' It's just that however obvious the answer is, we often fail to either admit or believe it. Martin Luther is said to have admonished the Dutch philosopher Erasmus: 'Your thoughts of God are too human.'[5] Jim Packer elaborates:

> This is where most of us go astray. Our thoughts of God are not great enough; we fail to reckon with the reality of his limitless wisdom and power. We think of God as too much like what we are. Put this mistake right, says God; learn to acknowledge the full majesty of your incomparable God and Saviour.[6]

And the main reason our God is 'incomparable' is because, as he reminds us in this verse, of his holiness. Indeed, in the Hebrew text, God is referred to as 'Holy One', without the definite article, thereby accentuating that this is who God is, not merely what God is. As one commentator puts it: 'Only God can ask these questions for only God is holy. [Mankind] is finite, temporal and, because of sin, mortal; God is infinite, eternal and unchangeable.'[7]

But our God is not only the Holy One, he is also the Creator. Go outside on a clear night says Isaiah (v. 26)— away from the towns and cities—and look up and see the stunning display of God's glory. Did you know that there are something like a trillion stars in our galaxy alone and there are getting on for a trillion galaxies making around a septillion (10^{24}) stars in the universe? That's more stars than grains of sand on planet earth. Did you know the nearest star to earth—apart from the sun—is 39.9 trillion kilometres or 4.2 light years away? And a light year is about 6 trillion miles! I could go on, but even with those scant statistics, contemplate the words of verse 26. Do you think that the God who 'brings out their host by number, calling them all by name ... not one of them is missing' will lose track of you? No! This God is deserving of both our confidence and our worship.

FOR FURTHER READING: ISAIAH 40

Reflect on these points:

1. 'Our thoughts of God are not great enough; we fail to reckon with the reality of his limitless wisdom and power. We think of God as too much like what we are' (Jim Packer).

2. Do you think that the God who 'brings out the host [of the stars] by number, calling them all by name ... not one of them is missing' will lose track of you?

3. However obvious the answers are to God's questions, we often fail to either admit or believe them.

Come—freely!

Chapter 7

Why do you spend your money for that which is not bread, and your labour for that which does not satisfy?

Isaiah 55:2

God opens the fifty-fifth chapter of Isaiah with this invitation: 'Come, everyone who thirsts, come to the waters; and he who has no money, come buy and eat! Buy wine and milk without money and without price' (Isaiah 55:1). And there are three things we need to notice about this invitation. First, that it's for 'everyone' (v. 1). As a book, Isaiah is mostly directed at the kingdoms of Israel and Judah. It's their kings that are mentioned, their history that is told, their future exile that is prophesied. But early in the book, there are glimpses of a coming Messiah—that he would be born of a virgin and called Immanuel (Isaiah 7:14), that he would have divine titles (9:6), and that he would be of the royal line of David (9:7). But then we discover that Messiah will not be a king in the usual sense but a Servant who will suffer—he will be 'despised and rejected by men, a man of sorrows and acquainted with grief' (53:3), he will be put to death (53:7–9), but will rise again (53:10–11). Moreover, he will come not just to Israel, but for 'many peoples' (2:3) and for 'the nations' (9:1). The apostle confirms this in what may be one of the Bible's best-known verses: 'For God so loved the world, that he gave his only Son, that whoever believes in him should not perish but have eternal life' (John 3:16).

Second, the invitation is not only for all, it's free. 'Come, everyone who thirsts, come to the waters; and he who has no money, come, buy and eat! Come buy wine and milk without money and without price' (v. 1). To accept this invitation and 'buy' this food and drink, we need no money. There is nothing to pay. Let me try to illustrate that. Judge David N. Edelstein was a U.S. district court judge. Having met Judge Edelstein at a conference in 1983, I met him again whilst visiting New York a few years later, but this time I had some school students with me. Edelstein invited us all to lunch at the exclusive club he belonged to in Manhattan. He seated us at a table in the members' ornate dining room. Menus arrived—and our hearts sank. I could see that my students had seen what I'd seen—the prices! They were way beyond anything that we could afford. Edelstein looked across the table and in his rich Yankee accent boomed two words, 'Order freely!' We did just that and upon leaving paid not a cent. And God says to you, 'Come—freely!'

Now when things are 'free' they are often of dubious worth and quality. But not so with God's free gifts. He offers not only water but also milk and wine—and figuratively, these three have a rich biblical pedigree. In the Old Testament, water reminds us of the gracious and free provision to Israel when Moses was told by God to 'strike the rock and water will come out, and the people will drink' (Exod. 17:6). And in the New Testament we're reminded of Jesus' conversation with the Samaritan woman by the well when he tells her that 'everyone who drinks of this water will be thirsty again, but whoever drinks of the water that I will give him will never be thirsty again' (John 4:14). Milk is for our nourishment and in the Old Testament reminds us of the Promised Land (Exod. 3:8), whilst in the New Testament we are exhorted to 'long for the pure milk of the word, so that by it you may grow in respect to salvation' (1 Peter 2:2 NASB). Wine not only brings joyful exhilaration (Ps. 104:15) but is also a metaphor that Jesus uses for the gospel—what one commentator calls 'the new wine of rescue and riches for all who are willing to accept these blessings'.[1]

But although God's provision is made freely available to us, as with food in the New York club, someone has had to pay for it. And Isaiah has already told us who it is who has paid the price—the suffering Servant, the promised Messiah, the Lord Jesus Christ. And at what a cost to himself! 'But He was wounded for our transgressions, He was bruised for our iniquities. The chastisement for our peace was upon Him, and by His stripes we are healed' (53:5 NKJV).

And it's upon this free nature of the invitation that God asks his question in verse 2. It's clear from verse 1 that those who accept God's invitation are those who are spiritually thirsty and know they are spiritually poor. They recognise their sin and their consequent need of a Saviour and they know they have nothing to bring in payment. Is that you? But verse 2 introduces us to a second group of people—

probably the vast majority—who think they're spiritually okay. They have no sense of sin and therefore see no need of a Saviour. And God asks them: 'Why do you spend your money for that which is not bread, and your labour for that which does not satisfy?' And if you're trying to find your salvation in anything other than the gospel of the Lord Jesus Christ, God asks you the same question.

But not only is the invitation for all and entirely free, it's also guaranteed. God declares: 'And I will make with you an everlasting covenant, my steadfast, sure love for David' (v. 3). The word rendered here as 'steadfast, sure love' is the Hebrew word *hesed* which refers to the faithfulness of God—that his promises are sure, constant and never-failing. This promise—this covenant—was given to David when God promised him that 'your throne shall be established forever' (2 Sam. 7:16). As Richard Phillips points out, 'This promise must be fulfilled in one who possesses eternity as one of his personal attributes, which is true only of David's descendant and God's own Son, Jesus Christ.'[2] This is the guarantee of God's invitation to us of salvation and eternal life. And the angel announces this at the very moment when Jesus' birth is foretold when he says to Mary that 'the Lord God will give to him the throne of his father David, and he will reign over the house of Jacob forever, and of his kingdom there will be no end' (Luke 1:32–33).

Later, Jesus sets these verses from Isaiah 55 in their New

Testament setting in the parable of the Great Banquet in which the invitations go out, 'Come, for everything is now ready' (Luke 14:17). Elsewhere, we hear Jesus say, 'If anyone thirsts, let him come to me and drink' (John 7:37). And on the Bible's final page we read: 'The Spirit and the Bride say, "Come." And let the one who hears say, "Come." And let the one who is thirsty come; let the one who desires take the water of life without price' (Rev. 22:17). Come freely! Have you responded to this free invitation?

> I heard the voice of Jesus say,
> 'Behold I freely give
> The living water; thirsty one,
> Stoop down, and drink, and live.'
> I came to Jesus, and I drank
> Of that life-giving stream,
> My thirst was quenched, my soul revived,
> And now I live in Him. [3]

FOR FURTHER READING: ISAIAH 55

Reflect on these points:

1. *Now when things are 'free' they are often of dubious worth and quality. But not so with God's free gifts.*

2. *But although God's provision is made freely available to us, as with food in the New York club, someone has had to pay for it.*

Strength for
hard times

If you have raced with men on foot, and they have wearied you, how will you compete with the horses?

Jeremiah 12:5

President Ronald Reagan loved to tell anecdotes. One of his favourites during his 1984 re-election campaign was of a tourist arriving by taxi at the National Archives building in Washington DC who asked the cab driver what the inscription 'What Is Past Is Prologue' over the front portico meant.

'Oh that,' said the driver to the tourist, 'that's bureaucrat talk. What it really means is, "You ain't seen nothing yet!"'

That phrase became Reagan's favourite catchphrase of the campaign. And if you're puzzled by the meaning of the text at the head of this chapter, then think of it as if God said to Jeremiah: 'You ain't seen nothing yet!' But as usual, we need a bit of context.

Jeremiah began his preaching in Jerusalem, warning the people that unless they repented of their sins, the city would be destroyed. It wasn't what folk wanted to hear! And so in chapter 11, God reveals to his prophet that there's a plot to kill him. But most hurtful of all, it's people from his hometown of Anathoth who are hatching the plot. Indeed we even learn a bit later that the plotters included his own kith and kin, 'your brothers and the house of your father, even they have dealt treacherously with you' (12:6). 'Do not prophesy in the name of the LORD, or you will die by our hand' (11:21), is what they've been saying. This catches Jeremiah completely by surprise. 'I did not know it was against me they devised schemes,' Jeremiah tells us. He felt 'like a gentle lamb led to the slaughter' (11:19). Faithfully proclaiming God's Word can be a dangerous occupation. I can still remember the minister of the church we attended as a family being hit with an umbrella by a female member of the congregation who took exception to the biblical content of his sermons! Not quite death threats, but intimidating and unpleasant nonetheless.

Well, the result of all this is Jeremiah's complaint to God in the opening four verses of chapter 12. And Jeremiah asks God the age-old question: 'Why does the way of the wicked prosper? Why do all the treacherous thrive?' (v. 1). Jeremiah is deeply concerned with such matters—and so often are we. He's not the first to ask such questions. Job asked them centuries before Jeremiah:

> Why do the wicked live,
> reach old age, and grow mighty in power?
> Their offspring are established in their presence,
> and their descendants before their eyes.
> Their houses are safe from fear,
> and no rod of God is upon them.

(Job 21:7–9)

The psalmist Asaph wrestled with the same problem:

Behold, these are the wicked;

always at ease, they increase in riches.

(Psalm 73:12)

In other words, why do good things happen to bad people? And there seem to be only two plausible answers: either God is not sovereign, or God is not good. But if one believes in the God of the Bible—who is both sovereign and good—this is a problem. Jeremiah knows that God is sovereign. Look at verse 2, 'You plant them, and they take root; they grow and produce fruit.'

And when we are thinking or saying these kind of things, we need to be on our guard—for a number of reasons. First, such thoughts can all too easily lead to self-pity. That's what Asaph descended into in the first half of Psalm 73. Second, we can get anxious, even envious—especially if we start to doubt God's sovereign goodness. In such situations we need to hear and heed the psalmist's advice: 'Fret not yourself because of evildoers; be not envious of wrongdoers!' (Psalm 37:1). Third, we need to guard against always thinking we know—or want to know—all the answers. That was what was wrong with Job's so-called comforters. They thought they knew all the answers to the whys and wherefores of life, but they were wrong and so can we be. When, like Jeremiah, we think that God is being dilatory (v. 4), we need to remember, as one commentator helpfully puts it, that God's seeming unwillingness to deal with the wicked 'does not have anything to do with God's ignorance of the situation. Neither does it have anything to do with his ability. God is not ignorant; he knows everything. God is not impotent; he can do anything. The issue is God's plan and God's timing.'[1]

God is infinitely patient with us, even when we are mistaken, just as he is with Jeremiah. But we need to notice that God doesn't reply to Jeremiah's complaint with a pat answer. As Derek Kidner puts it: 'God's answer is never philosophical, as though he owed us explanations, but always pastoral, to rebuke us, re-orientate us or reassure us.'[2] Rather, he asks a question of his own—or rather two questions, both somewhat cryptic. And that brings us to our text in verse 5. These are the questions God poses:

> If you have raced with men on foot, and they have
> wearied you,
> how will you compete with horses?
> And if in a safe land you are so trusting,
> what will you do in the thicket of Jordan?[3]

Let's take them in turn. In the first question, God is asking as it were, 'If you're tired running in the 1500 metres, how are you going to compete in the Derby?' And the second poses the same point in a different way: 'If you stumble walking along The Mall, how are you going to walk the Pennine Way?' Or, for my American friends, 'If you struggle walking across a bit of the Kansas prairie, how are you going to walk across the Rockies?'

So God's answer isn't soothing or reassuring. And in

the midst of trials, his word to us is sometimes, 'You ain't seen nothing yet!' So in hard times, don't pray for easier times, but pray for strength to face all that may yet befall you. Sometimes we say, 'I just can't take any more.' But we're not always the best judge of that. Isaiah has a word of encouragement for us from the Lord in such moments. Read it, believe it and rest peacefully:

> He gives power to the faint,
> and to him who has no might he increases
> strength.
> Even youths shall faint and be weary,
> and young men shall fall exhausted;
> but they who wait on the LORD shall renew their
> strength;
> they shall mount up with wings like eagles;
> they shall run and not be weary;
> they shall walk and not faint.
>
> (Isaiah 40:29–31)

FOR FURTHER READING: JEREMIAH 12:1–6

Reflect on these points

1. *'Fret not yourself because of evildoers; be not envious of wrongdoers!' (Psalm 37:1).*

2. *God is not ignorant; he knows everything. God is not impotent; he can do anything.*

3. *In hard times, don't pray for easier times, but for strength to face all that may yet befall you.*

Who speaks for God?

Is not my word like fire, declares the LORD, and like a hammer that breaks the rocks in pieces?

Jeremiah 23:29

In a previous volume, I told the story of how Watergate conspirator Charles Colson turned to Christ and found grace and forgiveness that transformed the rest of his life. Around ten years after his conversion, Colson wrote a book the title of which gives us this chapter's title—Who Speaks for God? In it, he pointed out how different people today claim to speak for God, yet they give contradictory messages.[1]

In the time of the Old Testament prophet Jeremiah, one could have asked the same question: 'Who speaks for God?' Jeremiah was a true prophet. How do we know? First, he was commissioned by God (Jer. 1:4–19). Second, God told Jeremiah what to say. Flick through the first twenty-two chapters and see how many times you read the words 'thus says the LORD' or 'declares the LORD.' Third, Jeremiah loved God's Word for he tells God that 'your words became to me a joy and the delight of my heart' (Jer. 15:16). Fourth, Jeremiah practises what he preaches—a godly lifestyle that mourns over sin and wants others to follow the path of the one true God. The same is true today, except reading 'preacher' or 'teacher' for 'prophet'. The true preacher or teacher has responded to a calling and a commissioning from God, and both loves and lives out God's Word.

Now alongside the true prophet Jeremiah were the false prophets—and that's what the second part of chapter 23 is about. But before we go into the detail, just a quick bit of context. Jeremiah begins his prophetic work in the thirteenth year of Judah's King Josiah and continues for some forty years to the end of Zedekiah's reign which is when the Babylonian exile occurs (Jer. 1:2–3). After the fall of Jerusalem, Jeremiah remains there with the remnant, but when they, in disobedience to God, go off to Egypt they take Jeremiah with them (Jer. 42–43), and in all probability he dies there. In the chapters immediately prior to chapter 23, God has been addressing the last of Judah's failed kings—Zedekiah (21:3), Shallum (22:11), Jehoiakim (22:18) and Coniah (22:24).[2] And of the latter God decrees: 'Write this man down as childless, a man who shall not succeed in his days, for none of his offspring shall succeed in sitting on the throne of David and ruling again in Judah' (Jer. 22:30).

It sounds like 'curtains'—God's finished with them all. The end! But does this mean that God has torn up the covenant he made with David those centuries ago when he promised him that 'I will establish the throne of [your] kingdom forever' (2 Sam. 7:13)? No! For what do we read of in the very next chapter? The promise of 'a righteous Branch' (23:5), who will save his people and whom God as the Good Shepherd 'will bring back to their fold' (23:3). Here is God's promise of not just a king but *the King*—the Lord Jesus Christ. God always keeps his promises.

But then suddenly in verse 9, our focus is taken back to the problem of the day—the false prophets, those who claimed to speak for God but had 'no message, no mission and no mandate'.[3] And then, as now, false teachers can so easily confuse and lead astray the people of God and we need to be constantly on our guard. We saw earlier the characteristics of a true prophet, so what are the characteristics of a false prophet, or a false teacher?

First, their lifestyles are ungodly.[4] I remember as a student visiting an Anglican vicar at his home and was shown into his sitting room whilst he finished a meeting with someone else. For no particular reason I leafed through the magazines on the coffee table finding, hidden down the pile, at least one copy of a pornographic magazine. After a few Sundays, I found that the Bible was pretty much absent from his 'sermons' and we parted company. Nothing much had changed from Jeremiah's day—'both prophet and priest are ungodly' (v. 11).

Second, their content is delusionary. God says, 'Do not listen to the words of the prophets who prophesy to you, filling you with vain hopes' (v. 16). These are the Christian ministers who tell us only that 'God is love' and imply that providing we live a 'good life' God will be delighted to have you in his heaven when you die. 'They say continually to those who despise the word of the Lord, "It shall be well with you"; and to everyone who stubbornly follows his own heart, they say, "No disaster shall come upon you"' (v. 17). The sermons of these preachers are mostly bland and soothing platitudes mixed with philosophical witticisms.

Third, their authority is false. They either merely spout their own ideas (v. 25) or quote each other (v. 30). 'Mr X or Professor Y says it, so it must be true.' The fact that it contradicts God's Word doesn't trouble them. Are the sermons you hear and the Christian books you read authenticated by God's Word, or are they merely human wisdom? In the words of verse 28, are they straw or are they grain? Are they truly nourishing you with the Bread of Life (John 6:35)?

And it's against this background that God asks his question: 'Is not my word like fire, declares the LORD, and like a hammer that breaks the rocks in pieces?' (v. 29). And the answer is a resounding 'Yes!' The true Word of God is like fire for 'it refines God's people and consumes everyone else'.[5] The New Testament gives us a different picture when it states that 'the word of God is living and active, sharper than any two-edged sword' (Heb. 4:12). And the apostle Peter reminds us that 'the grass withers, and the flower falls, but the word of the Lord remains forever' (1 Peter 1:23 quoting Isaiah 40:8). So I must in closing ask, Is this your view of God's Word? Can you truly say with the psalmist, 'I have stored up your word in my heart, that I might not sin against you' (Ps. 119:11)? Have we heard Jesus' own words: 'Blessed are those who hear the word of God and keep it!' (Luke 11:28)? As Charles Colson concludes: 'Who speaks for God? He does quite nicely for Himself, through His holy and infallible Word— and the quiet obedience of His servants.'[6] May this be our prayer:

> Speak, O Lord, as we come to You
> To receive the food of Your holy word.
> Take Your truth, plant it deep in us;
> Shape and fashion us in Your likeness ...
> Cause our faith to rise, cause our eyes to see,
> Your majestic love and authority.
> Words of power that can never fail;
> Let their truth prevail over unbelief.[7]

FOR FURTHER READING: JEREMIAH 23

Reflect on these points:

1. *God always keeps his promises.*

2. *Are the sermons you hear and the Christian books you read authenticated by God's Word, or are they merely human wisdom?*

3. *Can you truly say with the psalmist, 'I have stored up your word in my heart, that I might not sin against you' (Ps. 119:11)?*

The Gospel according to Ezekiel

Chapter 10

Son of man, can these bones live?

Ezekiel 37:3

One of the most wonderful things in reading the Bible is to find the Christian gospel signposted in the Old Testament. We saw it earlier in Isaiah 55 and now we see it again in Ezekiel 37. But unlike Isaiah and Jeremiah, Ezekiel was a prophet of the exile (Ezek. 1:1). So unlike the earlier prophets, his ministry was not just to Judah or to the ten-tribe kingdom, but to 'the whole house of Israel' (36:10) and his purpose was to remind the generation born in exile of the national sins that had brought Israel so low and to sustain them with God's promises of future restoration. It's this theme of national restoration that is the focus of chapters 36 and 37. In chapter 36, God has made some wonderful promises to his people:

> I will sprinkle clean water on you, and you shall be clean from all your uncleannesses, and from your idols I will cleanse you. I will give you a new heart, and a new spirit I will put within you. And I will remove the heart of stone from your flesh and give you a heart of flesh. And I will put my Spirit within you, and cause you to walk in my statutes and be careful to obey my rules.(Ezek. 36:25–27)

Jesus will give these verses a gospel context when he tells Nicodemus that 'unless one is born of water and the Spirit, he cannot enter the kingdom of God' (John 3:5). The chapter in Ezekiel ends with a vision depicting flourishing garden cities 'filled with flocks of people' (Ezek. 36:38)—truly vibrant and living. So the opening of Ezekiel 37 comes as a real shock!

In these verses, we are confronted with an exiled people who are lost, hopeless—and for all intents and purposes—dead. Indeed, in verse 11, God repeats to Ezekiel what these people are saying: 'Our bones are dried up, and our hope is lost; we are indeed cut off.' Let's consider it in four parts: the scene; the question; the means; the miracle.[1]

The scene (vv. 1–2) is a gruesome one—'the unburied, skeletal remains of a fallen army'.[2] The valley in which the vision is set is 'full of bones' (v. 1) of which there are 'very many' (v. 2). And they're very dead and 'very dry'. It doubtless looked like the scene following a great and bloody battle after which the slain have remained unburied—the final insult.

It's against this horrific and seemingly hopeless scene that God asks his question of Ezekiel: 'Son of man, can these bones live?' (v. 3). Most of God's questions that we have considered thus far have remained unanswered by the person or people to whom they were addressed. The only people to answer God's questions have been Cain, Elijah and Isaiah, and of these three of only Isaiah can we be certain that he answered faithfully.[3] Well, Ezekiel's answer is remarkable—what Alexander Maclaren calls, 'a noble utterance of faith and submission'—'O LORD God, you know' (v. 3).[4] Maclaren continues: 'Presumption would have said "Yes"; Unbelief would have said "No"; Faith says "You know".'[5] Ezekiel, as it were, took God's own words to Abraham and replied, 'Is anything too hard for the LORD?' (Gen. 18:14). No! For as Jesus himself said: 'With man this is impossible, but with God all things are possible' (Matt. 19:26). Indeed, centuries earlier, God had told Moses: 'I kill and I make alive; I wound and I heal' (Deut. 32:39). But how will God do it?

That brings us to our third part—the means by which God acts. And we find in verses 4–10 that God converts the dry bones of verse 2 into the living army of verse 10 by the power of his Spirit. It's not obvious in English that these verses are permeated with one Hebrew word—*rûah*. It comes eight times—translated in the ESV as 'breath', 'wind' or 'winds'. Significantly, it's the same word rendered 'Spirit' in verses 1 and 14 which bookend this passage. So what we have here is a play on words. We can read verse 5, for example, as 'Behold, I will cause the Spirit to enter you, and you shall live,' or verse 10 as, 'And the Spirit came into them, and they lived.' Greek also uses the same word for breath, wind and spirit—*pneuma*. And that's the word the apostle John uses in his gospel when Jesus says to Nicodemus: 'The wind (*pneuma*) blows where it wishes, and you hear its sound, but you do not know where it comes from or where it goes. So it is with everyone who is born of the Spirit (*pneumatos*)' (John 3:8). So whereas the immediate context of these verses is, as God himself explains in verses 11–14, that God's exiled people will return, revived, to their own land, the broader context is to signpost the gospel message that God can, and will, revive those who were spiritually dead by the power of his Holy Spirit. So Ezekiel's vision points us forward to the apostle Paul's description of the unregenerate person: 'And you were dead in the trespasses and sins in which you once walked' (Eph. 2:1), and of how 'even when we were dead in our trespasses' God 'made us alive together with Christ' (Eph. 2:5). So this passage really is the gospel according to Ezekiel!

Finally, there is the miracle itself—a miracle in two parts. In verse 4, God tells Ezekiel to 'prophesy over these bones, and say to them, O dry bones, hear the word of the LORD.' In verse 7, Ezekiel does just that. What's the result? A sound, a rattling, the bones come together, then sinews, flesh and skin cover them (vv. 7–8). 'But', records the prophet, 'there was no breath (*rûah*) in them' (v. 8). So had God failed? Was the answer to the question in verse 3 a negative? But before Ezekiel could even have the thought, God speaks again (v. 9), telling Ezekiel to command the breath (*rûah*) to 'breathe on these slain, that they may live.' And again, Ezekiel obeys (v. 10), 'and the breath (*rûah*) came into them, and they lived and stood on their feet, an exceedingly great army.'

Now we've already said that this passage should get

us looking forward in our Bibles, but now we find that we should also be looking back—to Genesis 2, and God's creation of mankind. For when God created Adam in Genesis 2, that was also a two-stage process involving first his formation (Gen. 2:7a) and then his being filled with the breath of life (Gen. 2:7b). So here we have two signposts— one back to mankind's human birth, and another forward to mankind's spiritual rebirth. And the miracle that God still performs today is to transform dead souls into living, breathing, Spirit-infused children of God—through the power of his Spirit. Has he worked that miracle in your life? Have you made this hymn your prayer?

> Eternal Spirit, by whose breath
> The soul is raised from sin and death,
> Before Thy throne we sinners bend;
> To us Thy quickening power extend.[6]

FOR FURTHER READING: EZEKIEL 37:1–14

Reflect on these points

1. *'Presumption would have said "Yes"; Unbelief would have said "No"; Faith says "You know"' (Alexander Maclaren).*

2. *The miracle that God still performs today is to transform dead souls into living, breathing, Spirit-infused children of God—through the power of his Spirit.*

What is true religion?

Chapter 11

When you fasted and mourned … was it for me that you fasted?

Zechariah 7:5

Motives are important, especially when it comes to matters of religion. A recent opinion poll in the United States asked folk why they went to church. The most popular reasons included: to give their children a good moral foundation; to become a better person; to continue family traditions; to meet new people and socialise.[1] (In passing, one might add that the most important reason for going to church is because Almighty God is worthy of our praise and he both deserves and demands our worship. It's about him, not us.) It's motive that's at the centre of Zechariah's sermon in chapters 7 and 8 of the Old Testament book that bears his name. But first, a quick bit of context.

Zechariah, along with his contemporary Haggai, is a prophet of the restoration after the exiles returned from Babylon. The book covers a period of around two years during the reign of King Darius, reminding us that although the Jews were back in their own land they were still under foreign rule. When chapter 7 opens—'in the fourth year of King Darius' (v. 1)—scholars estimate that we're in December, as it were, of 518 BC. We know from Haggai that the rebuilding of the temple had begun two years earlier and would take around five years to complete.

So the work must have been reaching the halfway stage when the delegation from Bethel arrived in Jerusalem in verse 2 with a question about fasting.

God had ordained only one annual fast—on the Day of Atonement. But after the fall of Jerusalem the exiled Jews in Babylon had become somewhat obsessive about fasting and mourning. Two extra fasts are mentioned in this chapter (v. 5) and chapter 8 mentions two more (v. 19). The one that the Bethel delegation ask about is the one in the fifth month that commemorated the destruction of the temple by Nebuchadnezzar. So now the temple was being rebuilt, 'Should I weep and abstain in the fifth month, as I have done for so many years?' they ask the priests and the prophets (v. 3). There may be a hint of weariness in the final phrase—'for so many years'—but nonetheless it seemed a reasonable question to ask. But before the temple hierarchy could come up with an answer we read in verse 4 that 'the word of the LORD of hosts came' to Zechariah giving not an answer, but posing a question. 'When you fasted and mourned in the fifth month and in the seventh, for these seventy years, was it for me that you fasted?' (v. 5). Indeed, what God literally says is, 'Were you fasting for me, even for me?' As John Mackay rightly points out: 'God's question is not focusing on the origins of their fasts, but on the religious motivations behind them.'[2] Then God adds a supplementary question: 'And when you eat and when you drink, do you not eat for yourselves and drink for yourselves?' (v. 6). Their religion was self-centred not God-centred. In other words, their motives were wrong.

When it comes to distinguishing between dead religion and true worship, motive is an important factor. When we worship God, study the Bible, pray, fast—or whatever it is—why are we doing it? God had already given some very clear instructions about how his people should approach fasting. As he continues in verse 7: 'Were not these the words that the LORD proclaimed by the former prophets, when Jerusalem was inhabited and prosperous?' So what had God said through the pre-exilic prophets? Some two centuries earlier, in the time of Isaiah, the Israelites were asking God why he seemed to be ignoring their fasting: 'Why have we fasted, and you see it not? Why have we humbled ourselves, and you take no knowledge of it?' (Isaiah 58:3). And God replied that what was wrong was at the same time they were making a big show of their fasting, they were still quarrelling and fighting (v. 4). God went on to tell them that what he wanted to see was fasting hand-in-hand with a godly and sanctified life— freeing the oppressed, feeding the hungry, housing the homeless, clothing the naked (vv. 6–7). The sad thing was that despite all they'd been through in those two hundred years, they were still doing exactly the same thing! God tells them now, through Zechariah, that he wants their fasting to be centred on him, not on themselves, and he wants it to go hand-in-hand with that sanctified life—rendering true judgements; showing kindness and mercy; not oppressing the widow, the fatherless, the stranger or the poor; and not devising evil against one another in their heart (Zech. 7:9–10).

God hates our dead, hypocritical religion just as much as he hated it in Israel all those centuries ago. How easy it is for us to do all the right things, say all the right words, go through all the right rituals but for it to have absolutely no effect on our hearts or on our lives. God still says to us as he said to his people of old:

> He has shown you, O man, what is good;
> And what does the LORD require of you
> But to do justly, to love mercy,
> And to walk humbly with your God.
>
> (Micah 6:8 NKJV)

So what does true religion look like? Richard Phillips in his commentary on these verses in Zechariah suggests that it has three necessary ingredients: a desire for God himself, for his pleasure and glory; a concern for the inner realities of sin and righteousness, and only then with external blessings; it draws from the God's Word—hearing, believing and doing according to what God has spoken in his holy, inerrant and life-giving Word.[3] As for false religion, false spirituality, Martyn Lloyd-Jones puts it like this:

> We may be highly religious, but there may be no

place for God; or even if he does come in, he is simply there as someone who may be of help to us. We are at the centre of our religion; our religion is a religion without God. And that is, I suppose, the last, and the ultimate, sin.[4]

If that is you, then pray from the depth of your heart this ancient prayer of Archbishop Thomas Cranmer (1489–1556):

> Lord of all power and might, who art the author and giver of all good things: Graft in our hearts the love of thy name, increase in us true religion, nourish us with all goodness, and of thy great mercy keep us in the same; through Jesus Christ our Lord. Amen.[5]

FOR FURTHER READING: ZECHARIAH 7

Reflect on these points:

1. *How easy it is for us to do all the right things, say all the right words, go through all the right rituals but for it to have absolutely no effect on our hearts or on our lives.*

2. *True religion has three necessary ingredients: a desire for God himself, for his pleasure and glory; a concern for the inner realities of sin and righteousness, and only then with external blessings; it draws from the God's Word—hearing, believing and doing according to what God has spoken in his Word.*

Right and wrong judging

Chapter 12

Why do you see the speck that is in your brother's eye,
but do not notice the log that is your own eye? Or how
can you say to your brother, 'Let me take the speck out
of your eye' where there is a log in your own eye?

Matthew 7:3–4

Good teachers ask good questions. And Jesus as the supreme Teacher asks the very best questions some of which will be the focus of the remaining twenty chapters of this book. In his Gospel alone, Matthew records some eighty questions that Jesus asks—of the Pharisees, of his disciples both individually and collectively, of various people whom he meets and even of his Father (Matt. 27:46), as well as those that he asks through the parables he told. The first recorded questions of Jesus in Matthew come during the Sermon the Mount, and that is the setting for our lead text.

It's important to understand that this sermon is directed not at the crowds—although they were as it were eavesdropping on it—but at his disciples (Matt. 5:1–2). This, therefore, is not a list of suggestions addressed to anyone who fancies living a 'good' life but is the King's teaching for the King's disciples—which today means all true believers—on Kingdom living and runs through chapters 5–7 of Matthew's Gospel.[1] Indeed, these verses at the start of chapter 7 contain echoes of earlier teaching in the sermon. So here we have, as it were, the reverse of

Jesus' positive teaching in Matthew 5:7—'Blessed are the merciful, for they shall receive mercy'—as well as more detail on the fifth petition of the Lord's Prayer, 'Forgive us our debts, as we also forgive our debtors' (6:12). So in order to understand the significance and application of Jesus' two questions in verses 3 and 4, let's take a closer look at the first five verses of Matthew's seventh chapter.

'Judge not, that you be not judged', directs Jesus in verse 1. This is one of those Bible verses often quoted out of context by those who don't take the Bible seriously. Whenever a believer says something is morally wrong, they will often be told, 'Ah, but the Bible says you mustn't judge!' But is that what Jesus meant? Clearly not. After all just five verses later, Jesus tells his disciples not to 'give dogs what is holy, and do not throw your pearls before pigs'. And that must involve some judging.

There are examples of this sort of behaviour in the Bible itself. It's what the Pharisees were doing to Jesus. But it's also one of the issues raised in the account of when the prophet Nathan visits King David in 2 Samuel 12. David has just committed adultery and murder. Having spied Bathsheba, the wife of Uriah, bathing, David has an adulterous relationship with her. He then schemes to have Uriah put 'in the forefront of the hardest fighting' so that 'he may be struck down, and die' (2 Sam. 11:15)—which is exactly what happens. Once Bathsheba has observed the mourning period for her husband, 'David sent and brought her to his house, and she became his wife and bore him a son' (2 Sam. 11:27).

Against that background, Nathan is sent by God to rebuke David. And Nathan does this by telling David a story which is fictitious, but David believes to be true. Nathan tells of a rich man who has 'very many flocks and herds' and a poor man who has 'nothing but one little ewe lamb' which was so precious it was 'like a daughter to him.' A traveller visits the rich man but rather than kill one of his flock to feed him, he takes the poor man's only lamb to provide food for his guest (2 Sam. 12:1–4). 'Then David's anger was greatly kindled against the man, and he said to Nathan, "As the LORD lives, the man who has done this deserves to die"' (2 Sam. 12:5). The rich man who has stolen a lamb deserves to die, pronounces the King who has just stolen a wife and killed her husband for his own gratification. It's at this point that Nathan announces to David, 'You are the man!' David has unwittingly past sentence on himself.

And Jesus says: 'Judge not, that you be not judged. For with the judgement you pronounce you will be judged, and with the measure you use it will be measured to you.' David had a log in his own eye but thought he could see clearly to remove the speck that was in the rich man's eye. As A.W. Pink comments: 'What a strange thing the heart of the believer is! What a medley dwells within it, often filled with righteousness indignation against the sins of others, while blind to its own!'[2] Hence Jesus' double question in Matthew 7:3-4.

So what Jesus is warning us of here is wrong judging. He's forbidding a critical spirit, not the use of our critical faculty. He means it is wrong to concentrate our attention on the comparative minutiae of our fellow Christian's sin while ignoring the enormity of our own. As William Hendriksen explains, what Jesus is condemning here is 'the spirit of censoriousness, judging harshly, self-righteously, without mercy, without love.'[3] I think it was my godly maternal grandmother who whenever she heard a harsh criticism being made of someone else would ask: 'Is it true, is it kind, is it necessary?' It's a good rule.

What is more, Jesus gives us four reasons why we should not judge in this manner. First, God is the ultimate judge and we ought not to usurp his role. As James reminds us in his epistle: 'There is only one lawgiver and judge, he who is able to save and to destroy. But who are you to judge your neighbour?' (James 4:12). Second, when we judge, we invite judgement in return upon ourselves—both from God and those around us. Third, since we cannot know what is in the heart of our fellow human beings, we ought to be reluctant to offer our critique of them. And fourth, this mindset so quickly leads to hypocrisy (v. 5). As G.B. Caird puts it: 'Pseudo-religion, which Jesus calls hypocrisy, is for ever trying to make other people better; and the cure for it is a mirror.'[4] We ought, therefore, first 'to look into the mirror of God's Word and see how it reflects into our hearts in order that we may be clear-sighted followers of Jesus.'[5] Only then can we fulfil another biblical instruction: 'Brothers, if anyone is caught in any transgression, you who are spiritual should restore him in a spirit of gentleness' (Gal. 6:1). So as we speak, may this be our prayer:

> Speak through us now, O Lord;
> Your truth alone we seek;
> According to Your Word
> Be all the words we speak.[6]

FOR FURTHER READING: MATTHEW 7:1–6

Reflect on these points:

1. What Jesus is condemning here is 'the spirit of censoriousness, judging harshly, self-righteously, without mercy, without love' (William Hendriksen).

2. 'Pseudo-religion, which Jesus calls hypocrisy, is for ever trying to make other people better; and the cure for it is a mirror' (G.B. Caird).

3. What Jesus is warning us of here is wrong judging.

Have faith in God

Chapter 13

Do you believe that I am able to do this?

Matthew 9:28

In June 1859, a young Frenchman named Charles Blondin (1824–97) caused a sensation when he crossed Niagara Falls on a tightrope. The crossing—just over 300 metres long—took a little over seventeen minutes to complete. Thousands of spectators were there to watch. And as Blondin successfully completed the crossing, the crowds cheered ecstatically. He then repeated the stunt, this time pushing a wheelbarrow. The crowd roared even louder. Then his assistant climbed into the wheelbarrow and he set off a third time. The spectators held their breath. After what seemed like an eternity, they made it across—above the roaring waters of the falls. The crowd again went wild with appreciation. And above all the cheering, one voice could be heard yelling 'More! More!' Blondin held up his hand for silence.

'You want more, sir?' he asked.

'Yes, yes!' yelled the young man.

'Right then,' replied Blondin, 'step in.'

That's when trust is added to knowledge and assent to make true, saving faith.

Following the Sermon on the Mount, Matthew spends two chapters (8 and 9) narrating some of Jesus' miracles 'to show that Jesus not only has a great messianic message but also a great messianic mission.'[1] Matthew's account is not a comprehensive list—he includes some miracles that none of the other Gospel writers include, and omits others of which they give an account—but the Gospels are not just history. Yes, they are history, but that is not their primary purpose. Their primary purpose is theological and spiritual, and all the miracles have a theological and spiritual lesson to teach. Jesus' miracles have been variously categorised, but they mainly involve miracles over physical illness, the forces of nature, spiritual forces and even death itself. And in the ten miracles that Matthew narrates in these two chapters, he carefully selects examples of each. The passage from which our lead text is taken is found in the ninth of these ten accounts and concerns two blind men (Matt. 9:27–31) and is one that none of the other gospel writers include.[2]

In verse 27, Jesus is 'passing on' from having just raised Jairus' daughter from the dead when two blind men follow him. The phrase is significant, for although the Greek word Matthew uses can mean merely spatial movement, it's the same word he uses earlier in the chapter when he himself leaves his tax collector's booth and 'follows' Jesus (v. 9). And they start to call out: 'Have mercy on us, Son of David.' Now here's a term that is used in the Old Testament to refer to the promised Messiah and it's also the way that Matthew introduces Jesus to us in the very first verse of his Gospel ('The book of the genealogy of Jesus Christ, the son of David ...').[3] At last, someone has caught on to this truth! And they ask, not for healing or for sight, but for 'mercy'. Their cry indicates, therefore, that they believe that Jesus is God's man who shows God's mercy.

But their initial cry brings no response at all from Jesus. He seems to ignore them—passing on and eventually entering a house (v. 28). But like many others who call out to Jesus and are initially rebuffed or ignored, they're persistent—clearly following Jesus inside the house. And it's here that Jesus asks his question: 'Do you believe that I am able to do this?' Matthew makes no record of any specific reference—either by Jesus or by the two men—to what 'this' is. Literally, it's 'having mercy', but implicitly it's clearly referring to their having their sight restored.

So why does Jesus ask the question? Yes, they've called him 'Son of David', but do they understand what they've said? Do they truly believe their own words? And it's the same for you. It's relatively easy to mouth the words to well-known Christian hymns, songs, prayers and liturgies. It's easy to allow the right spiritual language to trip off your tongue. But do you truly believe it? God asks us the same question: 'Do you believe that I am able to do this?' And do notice carefully the question Jesus asks—it's about his ability, not his willingness, to do something. God does not guarantee to provide everything we want. He's not a heavenly butler! And these two answer in simple faith, 'Yes, Lord.' As one commentator writes: 'Their faith is small and imperfect, yet they have at least the seeds of full faith.'[4] So here's another reason why God might ask you a question—to give you the opportunity to articulate your faith in him. Then Jesus touches their eyes 'and their eyes were opened' (v. 30). So why does Jesus touch their eyes? He doesn't need to. But he does it first as a token of his love and mercy towards them, and second to affirm their faith that their seeing again was no coincidence, but a direct result of his healing touch.

But there are two important things we need to see here. First, that the means of this miracle was faith. 'According to your faith be it done to you,' says Jesus (v. 29). This does not mean that he heals as much as we believe. As Daniel Doriani so helpfully puts it: 'Faith does not merit Jesus' favour. Rather, faith claims his favour.'[5] So what is faith? It is not merely knowing that Jesus is the Son of God. Yes, there is a knowledge component to faith—understanding the doctrines of the gospel especially regarding what Christ accomplished on the cross—but faith's other two components are assent and trust; we must give personal assent to these doctrines and trust in Christ as our Saviour, another personal commitment. Yes, faith is only the means, but it is the only means.

Second, Jesus wants us to see the spiritual significance of his healing miracles. To that end, John in his Gospel often refers to them as 'signs'.[6] And these signs authenticated Jesus as God's promised Messiah and, indeed, as God. Throughout the Old Testament, the giving of sight is attributed only to God.[7] What is more, when Jesus miraculously gives sight to the blind, we're meant to see the spiritual parallel that he is the only one who can give spiritual sight to the spiritually blind, which is what we all are until God in his mercy opens our eyes and reveals himself to us. Indeed, God promises to give that gift to all who ask in faith.

> Just as I am—poor, wretched, blind—
> Sight, riches, healing of the mind,
> Yea, all I need, in Thee to find—
> O Lamb of God, I come.[8]

Jesus is spiritual heart-surgeon and optician, rolled into one—the one to whom we come in faith. He hears, he touches, he heals, for he is infinitely merciful.

FOR FURTHER READING: MATTHEW 9:27–31

Reflect on these points:

1. *It's relatively easy to mouth the words to well-known Christian hymns, songs, prayers and liturgies. But do you truly believe them?*

2. *God does not guarantee to provide everything we want. He's not a heavenly butler!*

3. *When Jesus miraculously gives sight to the blind, we're meant to see the spiritual parallel that he is the only one who can give spiritual sight to the spiritually blind.*

Recognising Jesus

Chapter 14

But who do you say that I am?

Matthew 16:15

Are you ever worried about not recognising people? Certainly failure to recognise someone who expects to be recognised can be distinctly embarrassing. Some years ago now, I was being shown around Georgetown University in Washington by a former pupil of mine. We came into an open square in front of the main building to find a man, casually dressed, with a group of students gathered round listening to him. We walked over and joined the group. The man was making some fairly party political points, and I—presuming he was a Georgetown professor—said to him, 'I'm very surprised that you're being so party political.'

'You don't know who I am, do you?' he said.

'No, I don't,' I replied, and then cheekily added, 'but then you don't know who I am either!'

Back came the reply: 'Well, I'm Arnold Schwarzenegger. Who are you?' You won't be surprised to hear that the conversation went no further! Not to recognise someone as well-known as a Hollywood film star can cause some embarrassment. But imagine failing to recognise God.

And that's what we have here in Matthew 16:13–14 when Jesus asks his disciples the first of two questions in this short passage. 'Jesus asked his disciples, "Who do people say that the Son of Man is?" And they replied,

"Some say John the Baptist, others say Elijah, and others Jeremiah or one of the prophets.'" Jesus is using the same technique he used earlier in Matthew 16—asking questions to develop the disciples' understanding. Now they focus on the more positive answers. John the Baptist—that's who Herod thought Jesus was back in chapter 14. Others thought he was Elijah, because of the prophecy in the penultimate verse of the Old Testament that God would 'send you Elijah the prophet before that great and awesome day of the LORD comes' (Mal. 4:5). Others thought Jesus was Jeremiah—maybe because like Jeremiah, Jesus employed verbal and visible parables, exposed Israel's sin, spoke against the temple, and warned of imminent judgement.

If I asked the same question today, I would likely get the contemporary equivalent answers: he was a prophet, he was a good man, he was a moral teacher. Most people fail to recognise who Jesus is because he came as a man; people don't want to admit that he's the unique Son of God. They may sing at Christmas, 'Veiled in flesh the Godhead see, Hail, the incarnate deity', but, sadly, they don't really believe it.[1]

And then in verse 15, Jesus asks his second, the big, question. Maybe of all the questions we shall hear Jesus ask in the Gospels, this is the most important, the most consequential of all of them. It's the one you really do need to be right about the answer. In the original, the 'you' is emphatic: 'You—who are you saying I am?' Peter realises that human categories are not sufficient for Jesus and answers in verse 16 with equal emphasis, literally: 'You—you and no other—are the Christ, the Son of the Living God.' Or as one of our Christian creeds puts it: 'Very God of Very God.'[2] But why is this so important? Because the value of Christ's work, his dying for sin, depends on who he is. If he's not God, then his death would have been of no more value than any other person's death—noble, but ultimately inconsequential. It's only because he is God that his death has infinite value and he is able to pay the penalty for our sin. Furthermore, because Jesus is God, he is the one who can show us God.

Peter's confession is the confession of every true Christian and of every true church. Indeed, as Jesus makes clear in the next few verses, it's the very foundation of both. So I'm bound to ask: is this your confession? Is this the very foundation of your faith? Is it the rock upon which your faith is built? For there is no other—as Jesus has already reminded us back in chapter 7 in his parable of the two builders—one building on the rock, the other on the sand—and only the former survives.

But then notice, if you will, in verse 17 how Jesus responds to Peter's confession. You see, his response is not, 'Well done, Peter, you've got it!' No—because Peter's confession, his declaration, is not a human achievement. 'Blessed are you, Simon Bar-Jonah!' says Jesus, 'for flesh and blood has not revealed this to you, but my Father who is in heaven.' Peter's declaration is by gracious divine revelation. And it's the same for us. We get to see who Jesus is only by divine and gracious revelation. Has God revealed that to you? Not, 'have you got there?' Not, 'have you made this great discovery?' As the apostle Paul sums it up in 1 Corinthians 2, 'What no eye has seen, nor ear heard, nor the heart of man imagined, what God has prepared for those who love him—these things God has revealed to us through the Spirit' (1 Cor. 2:9-10 quoting Isa. 64:4).

That's why we should pray for our family members and friends who don't as yet recognise Jesus Christ as their Lord and Saviour, that God will 'reveal himself' to them. And today, he does that through his Word—the Bible. As the nineteenth century hymn writer George W. Doane (1799–1859) put it:

> Thou art the truth—Thy word alone
> True wisdom can impart;
> Thou only canst inform the mind,
> And purify the heart.[3]

But we mustn't miss one other nugget in verse 17 when Jesus talks of 'my Father in heaven'—one of the clearest claims of Jesus to his deity. Indeed, he makes such claims again and again. And it's because of these claims that the answer to the 'Who is Jesus?' question that uses phrases like 'moral teacher' or 'prophet' are so ridiculous. As the Christian apologist C.S. Lewis put it so memorably:

> A man who was merely a man and said the sort of things Jesus said would not be a great moral teacher. He would either be a lunatic—on the level with the man who says he's a poached egg—or else he would be the Devil of hell. You must make your choice. Either this man was, and is, the Son of God, or else a madman or something worse.[4]

Not recognising Arnold Schwarzenegger can be momentarily embarrassing. Not recognising the Only Begotten Son of God will have eternal implications.

FOR FURTHER READING: MATTHEW 16:13–20

Reflect on these points:

1. *The value of Christ's work, his dying for sin, depends on who he is. If he's not God, then his death would have been of no more value than any other person's death. It's only because he is God that his death has infinite value and he is able to pay the penalty for our sin.*

2. *We get to see who Jesus is only by divine and gracious revelation.*

The value of
your soul

For what will it profit a man if he gains the whole world and forfeits his soul? Or what shall a man give in return for his soul?

Matthew 16:26

Peter has just established that Jesus is 'the Christ, the Son of the living God' (Matt. 16:16). Jesus immediately foretells his death and resurrection (vv. 21–23) and then lays out the three principles of Christian discipleship—deny oneself, take up one's cross, and follow Jesus (v. 24). Indeed, they are more than principles, they are commands. So what does Jesus mean? First, to deny yourself means to renounce the kingship of your life. It's the same word as Jesus uses when foretelling that Peter would deny him three times. Just as Peter disowned Jesus, so we are to disown ourselves. This isn't denying ourselves things; it's denying ourselves! Second, we are to 'take up our cross'. People often refer to burdens as 'a cross I have to bear'—a physical ailment, an irritable boss, noisy neighbours. This, most emphatically, is not what Jesus means. Dietrich Bonhoeffer (1906–45) famously said, 'When Christ calls a man, he bids him come and die.'[1] For Bonhoeffer, that meant standing against the Nazi regime in Germany which cost him his life. The cost may be just as dear in some countries today. For most of us it may well mean 'forsaking materialistic self-absorption in order to serve and give' to gospel work.[2] It is self-denial—

not in the sense of giving up cream cakes for Lent, but giving up the throne of our lives to Christ.

The apostle Paul writes: 'I have been crucified with Christ. It is no longer I who live, but Christ who lives in me. And the life I now live in the flesh I live by faith in the Son of God, who loved me and gave himself for me' (Gal. 2:20). Can you honestly say that is true of your life? That's what Christ commands. And third, we are to follow him. According to Daniel Doriani, in Matthew's Gospel to follow Jesus is 'to believe all Jesus says, to obey all he commands, and to make his life a pattern for ours—always remembering that we, as mere creatures, dare not imitate some actions of the God-man'.[3] To put all these three commands together is saying, and living, that 'Jesus is Lord'. And maybe the most important word in these commands is not 'take up', or 'deny', or 'follow', but 'me'!

Jesus then goes on in verse 25 to talk about our attitude to our life—whether we seek to 'save' it or 'lose' it. The option appears at first glance to be a no-brainer—of course, we'd want to save our life rather than lose it. But that's not quite what Jesus means. By attempting to 'save' your life, Jesus is talking about your trying to keep control of it, make decisions about it without reference to him, living only for the fading pleasures of this world. No, the pleasures themselves may not be wrong—holidays, money, sport, success, pleasure, happiness, good health—it's the 'living for them' that's the problem. And if you're honest, none of these is ultimately satisfying, none brings inner peace, and most importantly none prepares us for a heavenly eternity. And that's why Jesus points out so clearly that if you try to hang on to your own life and reject what God wants, you will lose all in eternity. On the other hand, as Michael Wilkins explains, 'the person who lets loose their own self-centred desires and accepts God's will for them discovers true life—salvation and righteousness and the fulfilment that they gain as they receive the reality of life in the kingdom of heaven'.[4]

Jesus then drives these points home with a question, what J.C. Ryle describes as 'one of the most solemn questions that the New Testament contains'[5]—'For what will it profit a man if he gains the whole world and forfeits his soul?' (v. 26). Ryle continues: 'It is a question so well known, and so often repeated, that people lose sight of its searching character; but it is a question that ought to sound in our ears like a trumpet whenever we are tempted to neglect our eternal interests.' And like a number of Jesus' questions, the answer is so obvious that it's not verbalised—and that answer is 'nothing'. There is absolutely nothing that you can gain—nothing that this fleeting and oft-deceiving world has to offer—that could make a worthwhile exchange for your soul. Jesus, indeed, accentuates the question by immediately asking a follow-up: 'Or what shall a man give in return for his soul?' And again, the answer is 'nothing'. The Greek word here rendered 'in return for' (*antallagma*) literally means 'in exchange for' and expresses something beyond comparative value.

So what is the point, asks Jesus, of acquiring all the world has to offer and yet failing to settle your account with God and be lost eternally? The story is told of friends gathering at a rich man's funeral. 'How much did he leave?' asks one. 'Everything!' replies another. Or as someone once put it: 'I've never seen a hearse with a trailer!' At the end of your earthly life, you will be measured by the health of your soul, not the wealth of your investments.

In 1929, an American, Marion E. Wade, founded a small home and office moth-proofing company. The business grew quickly and in 1954 it was renamed ServiceMaster as a residential and commercial cleaning company. Today it's a Fortune 1000 company and has over 7,000 franchised locations across the United States, employs 13,000 people and has a turnover of over $2.5 billion a year. But Wade was a committed Christian and always ran the company on Christian principles. He often quoted this short poem called 'Questionable Progress':

> Here's a thought for today that I bring you,
> Without preaching or sermon or text:
> If you're getting ahead in this world, just be sure
> You're not getting behind in the next![6]

His favourite motto, referring to his personal Christian faith, was, 'If you don't live it, you don't believe it!' Wade's life was changed by the fact that he was a Christian. Have your ambitions been changed by a personal encounter with the Lord Jesus Christ? Have you realised how precious your soul is—precious enough for God's one and only Son to come and die to pay the price to redeem it! That's how precious your soul is to God!

> O teach me what it meaneth,
> That cross uplifted high,
> With One, the Man of Sorrows,
> Condemned to bleed and die!
> O teach me what it cost Thee
> To make a sinner whole;
> And teach me, Saviour, teach me
> The value of a soul.[7]

FOR FURTHER READING: MATTHEW 16:24–28

Reflect on these points:

1. *People often refer to something as 'a cross I have to bear'—a physical ailment, an irritable boss, noisy neighbours. This, most emphatically, is not what Jesus means. It is self-denial—not in the sense of giving up cream cakes for Lent, but giving up the throne of our lives to Christ.*

2. *Maybe the most important word in these commands is not 'take up', or 'deny', or 'follow', but 'me'!*

3. *'If you don't live it, you don't believe it!' (Marion E. Wade).*

The caper at Capernaum

Chapter 16

Which is easier, to say, 'Your sins are forgiven you' or
to say, 'Rise and walk'?

Luke 5:23

When in the late-1940s a Tennessee teenager decided to take up singing lessons, his teacher told him to forget it because he 'had no aptitude for singing'. Aged 19, he failed an audition for a local singing quartet. Discouraged, the young man got a job as a truck driver but still tried to join local bands. When one advertised an opening for a vocalist, he applied. 'Stick to truck driving because you're never going to make it as a singer,' he was told after failing the audition. Less than two years later, this persistent vocalist broke onto the music scene as a star. His name? Elvis Presley! Persistence is often rewarded.

And in this wonderful—and at times almost comic— story captured here for us by Luke, the friends of the paralysed man are certainly persistent. Mark in his account places the story in Capernaum, in a house where Jesus frequently stayed. But on this occasion, the place was jam packed. It was quite a crowd, for Luke tells us that 'Pharisees and teachers of the law were sitting there, who had come from every village of Galilee and Judea and from Jerusalem' (Luke 5:17). Indeed, by the end of Luke's account, one wonders whether it's not these folk who are the real paralytics—sullenly 'sitting there'—as the once paralytic man dances off through the open door! But we're getting ahead of ourselves.

When they arrived, carrying their paralysed friend on a bed, there was just no way in. But they were persistent. So they climbed the outside stairway which was a common feature in such buildings, and which led them on to the roof. Now this roof seemed to be rather more substantial than the usual domestic roofing of the time. Luke tells us—with detail that accentuates the authenticity of his account—that this roof had tiles. But we can still imagine what must have happened between Luke's two matter-of-fact phrases in verse 19—that 'they went up on the roof' and then 'let him down with his bed through the tiles into the midst before Jesus'. Jesus is teaching to a packed house, when suddenly there's a scrabbling going on overhead. Then tiles start to be torn away—and presumably falling debris, on those posh guests that Luke has mentioned. Then faces appear through the roof—before a man is lowered on a bed! It is for this reason that Kent Hughes dubs this incident 'the Capernaum Caper'![1] Even on the basis of these events, the house guests would have had good reason to say, 'We have seen extraordinary things today' (v. 26).

J.C. Ryle rightly suggests that we need to recognise three miracles in these verses, not just one. And the first comes in verse 20 as Jesus forgives the man's sins. In his first words to the paralytic, to the casual reader Jesus seems to be missing the point of why he'd come. Surely he'd come for healing not to be talked to about his sins. Jesus recognises that sin—not physical paralysis—is the man's biggest problem. And it's the same for us. The apostle John reminds us, 'If we confess our sins, he is faithful and just to forgive us our sins and to cleanse us from all unrighteousness' (1 John 1:9).

Luke now records the response to Jesus' declaration of forgiveness—by the Pharisees, by the paralytic and by the people. The Pharisees' response is to accuse Jesus of blasphemy (v. 21). Their logic is impeccable. 'Who can forgive sins but God alone?' they ask. Good question. They knew, after all, that the Old Testament gave to no one— no priest, no prophet, no theologian—any authority to forgive sins. Such people could pronounce in God's name that God had forgiven, or would forgive, their sin. But, as David Gooding correctly points out, 'None had authority to pronounce forgiveness in his own name, as Christ had just done.'[2] So as Jesus is claiming to be God, in their eyes he must be guilty of blasphemy. Not for one moment did they consider the alternative conclusion—that Jesus is the eternal Son of God.

And that leads us to Jesus' second miracle—that he could discern the very thoughts of their hearts (v. 22). This is the God of whom David wrote in Psalm 139:4, 'Even before a word is on my tongue, behold, O LORD, you know it altogether.' David goes on to say that 'such knowledge is too wonderful for me' (Ps. 139:6). But if you're not a true child of God then it's not wonderful at all—it's positively frightening!

So Jesus, having published the Pharisees' thoughts to the crowd, then poses his question: 'Which is easier, to say, "Your sins are forgiven you," or to say, "Rise and walk"?' (v. 23). And like so many of Jesus' questions, no record is made of any answer. But the implication is that the first is 'easier' because, unlike the second, there's no immediate and obvious proof of falsehood. Tell someone their sins are forgiven and no one is expecting to see anything visible happen, but tell a paralytic to 'rise and walk' and unless you do so your reputation is in tatters.

That's why Jesus now performs his third miracle— the healing of the man's paralysis (v. 24)—that this final miracle may give visible proof to the validity of his miracle of forgiveness. 'And immediately,' records Luke, 'he rose up before them and picked up what he had been lying on and went home' (v. 25). He came carried on a bed, and left carrying the bed. He came through the roof and left through the door. And just as there is a theological significance in Jesus' miracles that give sight to the blind, so there is in his making the lame to walk, for 'walking' is how the New Testament often portrays the regenerate life of the true believer.[3] As Charles Wesley expresses it in one of his best-loved hymns:

> Hear Him, you deaf; His praise you dumb,
> Your loosened tongues employ;

You blind, behold your Saviour come;

And leap, you lame, for joy.[4]

So finally we see more responses to Jesus. The Pharisees' response had been to falsely accuse Jesus of blasphemy, but the once-paralysed man 'went home, glorifying God' (v. 26)—as did the remaining onlookers of whom Luke records that 'amazement seized them all, and they glorified God'. That is the only appropriate response to the One who is truly Saviour and Lord:

My gracious Master and my God,

Assist me to proclaim

And spread through all the earth abroad

The honours of Your name.[5]

FOR FURTHER READING: LUKE 5:17–26

Reflect on these points:

1. *'The problem of sin, though not apparent to the eye as paralysis, is the fundamental problem of humanity that Jesus came to counteract' (Donald Hager).*

2. *'Even before a word is on my tongue, behold, O LORD, you know it altogether' (Ps. 139:4). David goes on to say that 'such knowledge is too wonderful for me' (v. 6). But if you're not a true child of God then it's not wonderful at all—it's positively frightening!*

Not just saying
but doing

Chapter 17

Why do you call me 'Lord, Lord,' and not do what I tell you?

Luke 6:46

Charles Colson, a senior member of President Nixon's White House staff, was a hard drinking, bullying, profane man whom work colleagues hated and feared in equal measure. That was Chuck Colson in the 1960s and early-70s. But in 1979, Colson started an organisation which eventually became Prison Fellowship International with the stated aim of mobilizing Christians in their ministry to prisoners initially in America, but later expanding into Britain, Canada and Australia. Why the change? Well, in 1973, Chuck Colson came to a saving faith in Christ. Having served seven months in jail for his part in the Watergate cover-up, he started this Christian organisation which he then led for over forty years. As Jesus says in Luke 6:44, 'Each tree is known by its own fruit.' The reason why Colson's fruit changed so dramatically was because his heart was changed so dramatically.

Here at the close of Luke 6, Jesus is concerned that we've heard all his teaching—about the Sabbath, about how we treat others, about the hypocritical judging of others—yes, we've heard it all, but do we ever do anything about it? The danger is that we listen to God's Word the way we listen to a flight attendant's safety briefing before we take off on a plane. The shades come down, the newspapers go up, the headphones go on. And although our life might depend on it, we've heard it all before, and we let it all just wash over us. This is no new problem. You can read of people doing it in the Old Testament. Here is God speaking to the prophet Ezekiel: '[Your people] say to one another, each to his brother, "Come, and hear what the word is that comes from the LORD." And they come to you as people come, and they sit before you as my people, and they hear what you say but they will not do it' (Ezek. 33:30–31).

As you read Jesus' teaching in Luke 6, it does all sound so obvious, and probably very familiar. You hardly need a degree in horticulture to understand verse 44: 'For figs are not gathered from thorn bushes, nor are grapes picked from a bramble bush.' But then if it's so obvious, why do many who call themselves Christians look so little like Christ? That's the challenge! And Jesus is saying here that it's all about your heart—the word comes three times in verse 45. So what Jesus is saying is that according to the laws of spiritual horticulture, we produce the kind of fruit that reflects what's in our hearts. There's a causal link between the kind of people we are on the inside, and the lives we lead on the outside.

There was an excruciating moment during Donald Trump's 2016 presidential campaign when a video was released from some years before of Trump arriving at a studio to appear on the TV show Access Hollywood. In that video, Trump was heard laughing and boasting about the way he'd behaved towards women, using the most lewd language. But after the video had been widely shown, Trump issued the following statement: 'Anyone who knows me, knows that those words don't reflect the person who I am.' Well, I'm sorry Mr. Trump, but they do reflect—like a mirror—exactly the person you are, what's in your heart, and what you fill your mind with. But then you and I are little different except our secret conversations are not broadcast on YouTube. What we do and say, especially in our most unguarded of moments, shows us exactly what's in our hearts.

But does that mean that the life of a Christian will never exhibit any of the bad fruit? No, sadly not. Because our sinful nature is never entirely eradicated this side of heaven. But when I see that bad fruit in myself, it should immediately prompt me not to the self-justification of Mr Trump, but to humble heart-felt repentance. When I say something that's mean-spirited or unloving, I'm tempted to say: 'I'm sorry, I didn't mean that,' when what I should say in all honesty is: 'You know, I'm so sorry because that really is what I'm thinking. I'm just usually better at hiding it!' You see, the tongue is the sound system of our hearts.

So in verse 46 Jesus poses his question: 'Why do you call me, "Lord, Lord," and not do what I tell you?' There are people, says Jesus, who call me 'Lord'—they say they respect my teaching authority—but they don't show it by what they do. And sadly we see the same thing in the church today. Are you someone who calls yourself a Christian, you're seen in all the right churchy places, you use all the right language, but in your life you don't bow to Jesus' authority? You hear God's teaching in his Word, but you do nothing about it.

And it's to make this very point that Jesus goes on to tell the parable of the two builders each building their house, but on different foundations. The person who 'comes to me and hears my words and does them,' says Jesus, 'is like a man building a house, who dug deep and laid the foundation on the rock' (vv. 47–48).

In the Yorkshire town of Knaresborough there's a house called the House in the Rock. It was constructed in the late-1700s by Thomas Hill and it's a four-storey house built into a limestone cliff. It took Hill sixteen years to build it and 250 years later it still stands as an extraordinary monument to Hill's dedication to build a house that would last. Even the floods of the River Nidd that flow at the foot of the cliff can't touch it. That, says Jesus, is a picture of someone who hears my words and then acts upon them, building their life on the solid foundation of salvation in Christ alone. But, Jesus continues, 'the one who hears [my words] and does not do them is like a man who built a house on the ground without a foundation. When the stream broke against it, immediately it fell, and the ruin of that house was great' (v. 49). And this is the person who builds not on the foundation of faith in the Lord Jesus

Christ, but on superficial spirituality, on religious ritual, on a man-made religion of so-called good works. But, Jesus warns, it will ultimately collapse—either under trial or suffering in this life, or at the final day of judgement. Both kinds of people hear Jesus' words. The determining factor is whether or not you act upon them. And Jesus asks you that same question today: 'Why do you call me "Lord, Lord," and not do what I tell you?' Charles Colson, with whom we began, offered this challenge:

> What's desperately needed today is a call to action. It is to Christians to get serious about their faith that 'was once for all entrusted to the saints,' as Jude teaches. It is to understand it, so that you can live it![1]

FOR FURTHER READING: LUKE 6:43–49

Reflect on these points:

1. *Jesus is saying is that we produce the kind of fruit that reflects what's in our hearts. There's a causal link between the kind of people we are on the inside, and the lives we lead on the outside.*

2. *There are people, says Jesus, who call me 'Lord'—they say they respect my teaching authority—but they don't show it by what they do.*

Grace

Chapter 18

Now which of them will love him more?

Luke 7:42

Embarrassing scenes can occur at smart parties. Picture if you will this scene that occurred a few years ago at an embassy drinks reception for a departing diplomat. Smartly-dressed folk were huddled in small groups indulging in polite small talk, enjoying drinks and canapés. But unbeknown to one of the lady guests, a waiter had crept up silently behind her on the deep-pile carpet, so she had no idea that with her expansive right-arm gesture she would karate-chop the waiter's tray, and over a dozen glasses of Pimm's and fruit juice went crashing to the light beige-coloured carpet. The ambassador kindly insisted that 'there's really no problem'. But the sight of his wife's wine-drenched ankles, not to mention the new mottle-shade of the carpet, told a different story! Yes, embarrassing scenes can occur at smart parties.[1]

And here in his seventh chapter, Luke gives us one of those wonderfully graphic stories from a day in Jesus' earthly ministry. He's been invited to a smart dinner party at the home of Simon the Pharisee. Local custom would tell us that such a soiree would probably have been hosted in the open courtyard of Simon's home and it was not uncommon for uninvited folk to drop by and join in the conversation. And thus is set up this story of contrasts—

of two very different people, and their two very different responses to Jesus.

First there is 'a woman of the city, who was a sinner' (v. 37). What a way to be identified! The word 'sinner'—used both by Simon (v. 39) and Jesus (v. 47)—has clear sexual overtones. She was undoubtedly a notorious prostitute. Reading between the lines, it's fairly clear that this is not the first time she had met Jesus. The later exchanges suggest that she had, probably quite recently, heard Jesus' teaching and had responded in saving faith. Not that Simon would have known that. He must have been appalled to see her. And then things got even worse for Simon as the woman makes what he must have regarded as an embarrassing scene at his smart party. She opens an alabaster flask of ointment, wets Jesus' feet with her tears, wipes them with her hair, kisses his feet and then anoints them with the ointment! So what is this all about? It's about her being overwhelmed by the grace that Jesus had shown to a sinner like her. So she brings probably the most expensive thing she owns and pours it out at Jesus' feet.

Then there is Simon. And the Pharisee with a name is the complete opposite of the woman with no name whom we've just met. He was the host; she the gate-crasher. Where she had lived an immoral life, Simon was definitely moral. Where Simon was an insider climbing the social ladder, she was an outsider who wasn't on any ladder.

The Gospels are full of delicious ironies, and there are two in verse 40. First, having been told that Simon said all these things 'to himself' (v. 39), the very next phrase reads: 'And Jesus answering said to him ...' As the psalmist writes: 'Even before a word is on my tongue, behold, O LORD, you know it altogether' (Psalm 139:4). That's a prophet's insight! Second, Simon's thought was that Jesus couldn't be a prophet otherwise he'd know all about the woman. But 'not only did Jesus know what kind of woman was washing his feet, but he knew what kind of man was sitting across from him at the table!'[2] And he knows all about me and about you—even the unspoken bits.

So Jesus tests out Simon by telling him a parable of a moneylender who had two debtors—one owed him 500 denarii, the other fifty. And because both 'had nothing with which to repay, he freely forgave them both' (v. 42 NKJV). What a wonderful and remarkable statement of the gospel! You have 'nothing with which to repay' God for your sin's debt. It's not that you've got most of what you owe, or half of what you owe, or even a tenth—you have 'nothing' that can ever pay the debt of your sin. That's why we sing:

> Nothing in my hand I bring,
> Simply to Thy cross I cling.[3]

And:

> Just as I am, without one plea,
> But that Thy blood was shed for me.[4]

And it's at the end of this short parable that Jesus poses his question to Simon: 'Now which of [these two debtors] will love him more?' (v. 42). And sneering Simon gives his reply: 'I suppose the one who he forgave more' (v. 43 NKJV). The trouble was that Simon didn't really believe it—because he didn't really see himself as God's debtor. Oh yes, he knew that 'this woman' was 'a sinner'. What he didn't know was that the world contains only two types of people—big sinners, and even bigger sinners—and although he may not be the latter, he was certainly the former, and as such needed big forgiveness. As Jesus so aptly puts it: 'He who is forgiven little, loves little' (v. 47). And Simon 'loved little'. So although this is one of the few of Jesus' questions that receives a direct answer—and a correct one at that—the sad thing is that the person giving the answer didn't really believe it, and certainly didn't live as if he believed it. We're not made right with God by just knowing the right theology.

And lest we should think that the woman was saved by her works, Jesus in pronouncing her forgiveness adds, 'Your faith has saved you; go in peace' (v. 50). Her love was not the ground of the pardon she had come to seek, but the proof of the pardon she had come to acknowledge. She came to Jesus seeing the enormity of her sin and therefore she loved Jesus for the grace he lavished upon her. Whilst Simon's motto was, 'I do, therefore I am accepted,' her motto was 'I am accepted, therefore I do.' So which motto do you live by? How do you approach Jesus? What response do you make to him? Do you come loving him little, or loving him much—because you see the enormity of his love and grace for sinners? Can you truly sing from your heart:

> Wonderful grace that gives what I don't deserve,
> Pays me what Christ has earned then lets me go free.
> Wonderful grace that gives me the time to change,
> Washes away the stains that once covered me.
> And all that I have I lay at the feet
> Of the wonderful Saviour who loves me.[5]

FOR FURTHER READING: LUKE 7:36–50

Reflect on these points:

1. *'The fundamental contrast was this: only one of them believed that God had grace for sinners' (Philip Ryken).*

2. *You have 'nothing with which to repay' God for your sin's debt.*

3. *How do you approach Jesus? Do you come loving him little, or loving him much—because you see the enormity of his love and grace for sinners?*

Other refuge
have I none

Chapter 19

Where is your faith?

Luke 8:25

In October 1735 John Wesley set sail from Gravesend for the British colony of Georgia in North America. The Atlantic crossing took four months and the ship faced a number of violent storms. On 17 January 1736 Wesley recorded in his diary that 'the sea broke over us from bow to stern, and even burst through the windows of the cabin, and covered us all over'. A week later, another violent storm hit the ship and Wesley wrote in his journal, 'I could not but say to myself, "How is it that you have no faith?"'[1]

Well, the story that Luke recounts here in these four vivid verses has something in common with Wesley's experience. Yet it all begins so innocuously in verse 22 with Jesus suggesting a boat trip across the Sea of Galilee. Luke records, 'So they got into a boat and set out.' And I guess many of us can think of days that began innocuously, but ended in an event of life-changing proportions. In the morning we thought we were fit and healthy; in the afternoon we were told we had a serious and life-threatening illness. One day you were talking with a close friend or loved one; the next they're taken from you by sudden death.

Then in verse 23, Luke records that 'a squall came down on the lake'. 'Squall' hardly does justice to Luke's original. Literally, it's 'a hurricane of wind'. Matthew in his account uses the word seismos—an earthquake. It was as if the lake was being shaken. And anyone who's been in a boat in a storm and has felt the bow plunge like an elevator only to shoot toward the sky like a monster roller-coaster, can easily imagine the disciples' misery. Luke records towards the end of verse 23: 'the boat was being swamped, and [the disciples] were in great danger'.

How this can be like us as we feel swamped by the conflicts, the hardships, the stresses and strains of everyday life. Now if you're not a Christian believer, maybe you just pass it off as 'fate'—or as Doris Day used to sing: 'Que sera, sera, whatever will be, will be.' But as Christian believers, what's our reaction as our life is swamped? Some wrongly enter the Christian life thinking that in itself this will mean the end to the storms of life. God loves me, they think, and has a wonderful plan for my life. If I faithfully serve Christ, then all will go well for me. But that's not what the Bible tells us. And the storms of life reveal the truth about our hearts. You see, if we're obeying God merely to get something in return, then it's that something that really controls your heart, not God. And the truth is going to be revealed by your reaction whenever God doesn't give you what you really want. So what we need to learn is that the circumstances of our lives are not an accurate measure of our relationship with God. And God is far more interested in your holiness than in your happiness.

Or another way we can react as a Christian in difficult circumstances is to presume that we must have wandered off from God's plan for our lives. It must be a sign of his displeasure, and it certainly can't be what he planned for us. But it's worth noting another detail of these verses by asking ourselves the question, 'How did the disciples end up being on the lake in this storm?' And the answer is in verse 22. Jesus suggests they go over the lake in the boat, and—what comes next—'So they got into a boat and set out.' Do you see, the disciples didn't end up in the storm because of their disobedience to Jesus, but because of their obedience to him.

And then in verse 24, we have the disciples' reaction— they 'went and woke [Jesus] saying, "Master, Master, we're going to drown!"' At least they knew who to turn to—Jesus—and so should we. But given what the disciples had recently experienced of Jesus—a leper cleansed, a paralytic healed, a widow's son raised from the dead— 'we're going to drown!' is not really the appropriate response. Like us, they immediately assumed the worst. In a conversation with a Christian friend recently, I was overcome by a moment of unvarnished honesty and admitted: 'You know, my trouble is that I react to the storms of life as if God had let me down on every previous occasion!' Like Jacob in Genesis 42, I'm too quick to blurt out, 'Everything is against me!'—when indeed God is just about to be very gracious, yet again!

Well, we've had the disciples' reaction to the storm but what about Jesus' reaction? The second half of verse 24: 'He got up and rebuked the wind and the raging waters.' And with what result? Luke continues: 'The storm subsided and all was calm.' And in the instant calm and stillness that followed, two questions are posed—one by Jesus, one by the disciples. First, Jesus asks the disciples a question at the beginning of verse 25: 'Where is your faith?' It's a gentle rebuke—to them and to us when we display that same lack of trust in God's faithfulness to be able to see us through life's storms.

In the storm, the boat wasn't the only thing getting swamped and overwhelmed. Fear had overwhelmed the disciples' faith. And isn't the same so often true of us? Luke doesn't record the disciples' answer, maybe because there was no answer. So how would I answer—how would you answer—'Where is your faith?' For only one answer will truly be able to sustain us in every storm of life: that my faith is in the life, death and resurrection of the Lord Jesus Christ. Is that where your faith is—in the one who died for you and for me? I do pray so.

Which leads us to the second question—the one asked by the disciples of each other. Verse 25 again: 'In fear and amazement they asked one another, "Who is this?"' And in the next chapter Luke will record the answer they eventually give, 'The Christ of God.' Is that truly your answer?

But I never quite finished John Wesley's story. Do you remember, Wesley was utterly faithless and bereft as he faced that Atlantic storm. 'How is it that I have no faith?' he asked of himself. But just three years later, Wesley was truly converted and wrote of his faith in a hymn he translated written some years earlier by Johann Rothe (1688–1758) which contains the following verse:

> Though waves and storms go o'er my head,
> Though strength, and health, and friends be gone,
> Though joys be withered all and dead,
> Though every comfort be withdrawn,
> On this my steadfast soul relies—
> Father, Thy mercy never dies![2]

That's what true faith alone can sing.

FOR FURTHER READING: LUKE 8:22–25

Reflect on these points:

1. *Some think that being a Christian will mean the end to the storms of life. But that's not what the Bible tells us. And the storms of life reveal the truth about our hearts.*

2. *The disciples didn't end up in the storm because of their disobedience to Jesus, but because of their obedience to him.*

3. *Do you sometimes react to the storms of life as if God had let you down on every previous occasion?*

Whose neighbour am I?

Chapter 20

Which of these three, do you think, proved to be a neighbour to the man who fell among the robbers?

Luke 10:36

Much media coverage was given to the violence that erupted outside Anfield—the home of Liverpool F.C.—when the Manchester City team coach arrived for a Champions League match in April 2018. Bottles, bricks and lighted flares were amongst the objects thrown by Liverpool supporters at the Manchester City team coach as it arrived with the team and staff. What received much less media coverage was what happened after the match. As the Manchester City team were leaving Anfield, in a replacement coach, they noticed a female Liverpool supporter lying in the road having just been the victim of a hit-and-run accident. The City team asked the coach driver to stop to allow members of their medical team—still wearing their distinctive kit—to treat the woman's injuries until the emergency services arrived. One onlooker told the local press: 'They were amazing. It was the exact spot where the bus had been battered by bricks and bottles, but they didn't hesitate, and helped the poor girl out.'[1] We shall return to this story later.

Here in Luke 10 we have one of the best known parables of Jesus, that of the Good Samaritan. The thirteen verses that contain the parable constitute a question and answer session between a lawyer and Jesus. In verse 25, the lawyer asks: 'Teacher, what shall I do to inherit eternal life?' Luke adds that the lawyer asked the question 'to put Jesus to the test'. Not only is this unbiblical—'You shall not put the LORD your God to the test' (Deut. 6:16)—it is utterly foolish. And the question itself is bad theology. The gaining of eternal life is not about what you or I 'do'. Yet countless people start from the same false premise today.

Jesus immediately asks the lawyer a question: 'What is written in the Law? How do you read it?' (v. 26). In asking this, Jesus is trying to help him see that the way to eternal life is in God's Word, not in 'good works'. And in verse 27, he reels off the right Old Testament verses.[2] 'Good answer!' replies Jesus (v. 28), before adding the sting in the tail: 'Do this, and you will live.' What this shows is that it's possible to know the right answers to Jesus' questions without actually knowing what they mean and how they apply to you.

This is where the lawyer's argument—and sometimes ours—really goes off the tracks. For confronted with such a high moral bar, the only appropriate response is to get down on our knees in a prayer of repentance seeking God's mercy and grace. But that's not quite how the narrative continues! 'But he,' Luke writes, 'desiring to justify himself, said to Jesus, "And who is my neighbour?"' (v. 29). Oh yes, he's happy to love those who exist within a clearly defined and closely-drawn circle, but he wants Jesus to draw him some red lines, conveniently excluding those who God surely can't expect him to love. And aren't we often the same? Isn't our definition of 'neighbour' often comfortably parochial? So it's to prick this particular balloon that Jesus tells the parable (vv. 30–35).

The parable itself is exquisite with its poignant details. The victim is left half-dead. Then the priest and the Levite 'passed by on the other side'—a glance maybe, perhaps a thought of personal danger, but no stirrings of pity. And then, in sharp contrast, there is the selfless care of the Samaritan who 'had compassion' on the victim, 'bound up his wounds, pouring on oil and wine, set him on his own animal, brought him to the inn and took care of him'. And he did more, paying for the victim's stay before telling the innkeeper, 'Take care of him, and whatever more you spend, I will repay you when I come back.' You see, religion to the priest, the Levite—and the lawyer—was 'a set of restrictive regulations'. But to the Samaritan—and to Jesus—it's 'a boundless series of opportunities'.[3] Which is it to you?

Now, with the parable told, Jesus poses his second question to the lawyer: 'Which of these three, do you think, proved to be a neighbour to the man who fell among the robbers?' It's very similar to the question Jesus asked the Pharisee in our previous exposition. The answer is obvious, but will the giver of the answer see its implications? But notice too, that in asking it this way, Jesus has subtly changed the question from the one the lawyer had asked. The lawyer had asked the merely academic question, 'Who is my neighbour?' But Jesus now asks him the practical question, 'Which proved to be a neighbour?' The first question is based on selfishness; the second on love. 'The one fixes attention on men's claims on me; the other on my debts to them.'[4]

So in his final words, Jesus tries to move the lawyer—and us—from the theoretical to the practical: 'You go, and do likewise' (v. 37). And that's the point of the story—not racial reconciliation or improving cross-cultural relationships, good as they are. But Jesus wants you to see that a neighbour is someone you are, not something you have and that, for a Christian, neighbourly love is a whole way of life. As one commentator puts it:

> Neighbour is not a concept to be debated or defined, but a flesh-and-blood person in the ditch waiting to be served. You can't define your neighbour in advance; you can only be a neighbour when the moment of mercy arrives.[5]

And this speaks to us on two levels. First, it tells us to emulate the Good Samaritan. Jesus shocks the lawyer with a parable in which a semi-pagan foreigner might know more about the love of God than a devout Jew.

Which brings us back to our opening story. No, I'm not suggesting that the occupants of the Manchester City team coach had scriptural teaching in mind when they stopped to assist that Liverpool supporter. But surely it should concern us when those who do not even profess to be true disciples of Christ show more practical neighbourliness than those who do. But second, this parable shows us our deep need for the gospel. The lawyer wanted to know what to do to be saved. And Jesus teaches us that his is a law we cannot keep. So whatever the law may do for us, it is quite unable to make us love our fellow mankind:

> So may our hearts remember yet
> That cross where love and justice met,
> And find in Christ our fetters freed,
> Whose mercy answers all our need:
> Who lives and reigns, our risen Lord,
> Where justice sheathes her righteous sword.[6]

FOR FURTHER READING: LUKE 10:25–37

Reflect on these points:

1. *The gaining of eternal life is not about what you or I 'do'. Yet countless people start from the same false premise today.*

2. *Isn't our definition of 'neighbour' often comfortably parochial? So it's to prick this particular balloon that Jesus tells the parable.*

3. *Jesus wants you to see that a neighbour is someone you are, not something you have, and that for a Christian, neighbourly love is a whole way of life.*

Trite or contrite?

Chapter 21

*Do you think that these Galileans were worse sinners
than all the other Galileans, because they suffered in
this way?*

Luke 13:2

Of all the questions asked by Jesus that we have
considered so far, this is the first one to which Jesus
himself immediately gives an explicit answer. Others had
either received no answer at all, the answer was implied
but not stated or the answer was given by the person
of whom the question was asked. As posed today, the
question would come out something like this: 'How can
accidents and atrocities happen in a world where God is
supposed to be in charge?' This and similar questions were
asked after the 9/11 attacks in the United States in 2001,
after the Indian Ocean earthquake and tsunami on Boxing
Day 2004, and even during the Covid-19 pandemic.

Jesus has just been teaching about the urgent need for
timely repentance (Luke 12:54–59) when some folk in
the crowd tell Jesus of a gruesome atrocity perpetrated
by the Roman governor of Judea, Pontius Pilate. It would
appear (Luke 13:1) that Pilate had, on some pretext, sent
some of his forces into the temple, killed a number of
Galilean worshippers, and then mingled their blood with
that of the temple sacrifices. This would have been utterly
shocking to anyone, but especially to devout Jews. So why
did this happen to these unfortunate Galileans? In such

circumstances people often want two things: an answer and someone to blame. The first lesson to learn when we find ourselves confronted with such situations is to resist the temptation to come up with some trite answer—to make it appear as if we know all the answers even to the most difficult of questions.

Either explicitly or implicitly it would appear as if these folk who brought this report to Jesus thought they had the answer. It was simple. These particular Galileans were clearly grievous sinners and therefore this atrocity was judgement from God. Jesus puts their thoughts into words in his question: 'Do you think that these Galileans were worse sinners than all the other Galileans, because they suffered in this way?' (v. 2). We're meant to think that at that very moment a lot of thought balloons were appearing above people's heads saying, 'Yes! You bet!' So Jesus' succinct answer must have come as a bit of a shock, 'No, I tell you' (v. 3). These folk believed rightly in God's providential governance but drew the wrong conclusion from it. Today the humanist sees 'bad things' happening to 'good people' and concludes, wrongly, that the unfairness proves their contention that there is no God. But both interpretations are based on the false premise that there are 'good people' and 'bad people'. And to deduce the right lesson we need the right theology, namely that we are all sinners—guilty without excuse before a holy God—and therefore the greater wonder is that any one of us survives another day.

So what are we meant to do in the face of human atrocities, natural disasters and individual suffering? First, avoid trite answers. We need to stop either appearing to put God on trial by accusatory questions and—at the other end of the spectrum—giving the impression that we have God all worked out. We need some intellectual and spiritual humility. 'The secret things belong to the LORD our God, but the things that are revealed belong to us and to our children forever' (Deut. 29:29), is how God expressed it to Moses. There are questions to which—this side of heaven—we shall never know the answer. We do not sit in judgement on God; he sits in judgement on us.

Second, we need to avoid taking good theology but then misapplying it. The Bible does record some natural disasters and tell us that they were acts of divine judgement. The perishing of the Egyptians in the Red Sea is a case in point. But we cannot from these few examples then assume that every natural disaster or calamity is therefore an act of divine judgement on somebody. Indeed, the Bible often warns us against such false deductions.[1]

So if these are some of the reactions we're meant to avoid in such circumstances, what lessons are we meant to draw? Firstly, such situations and events are meant to remind us that we all live under the shadow of death. Without wishing in any way to minimise the utterly awfulness of it, mass human tragedies—tsunamis, terrorist attacks, pandemics and the like—don't actually increase the death rate. It's still 100 percent. The death of any human being can be used by God to remind us of our own mortality.

And secondly, that should lead to the very point that Jesus goes on to make in these verses, that 'unless you repent, you will all likewise perish'. To put it another way, rather than be trite, we should be contrite. Repentance involves both a confession of our sin to God but also a sadness and remorse—'not just because we got caught, or have to face the consequences, but because we are grieved by our sin itself as an offense against God'.[2] And 'perish' takes us beyond death—not just that we may suffer some equally ghastly fate, but that we shall suffer the eternal wrath of God. That truly is a fate worse than death!

Thirdly, it is entirely appropriate to be indignant about death. The Bible teaches that death is wrong; it's not what God originally planned for his creation. Jesus was indignant as he stood at the tomb of Lazarus—he was 'deeply moved in his spirit' (John 11:33). Indeed, the Greek word here is the same word used in Mark 14:5 when Mary pours a jar of ointment over Jesus' head and some of the bystanders 'rebuked her harshly'. The American theologian Richard Phillips tells of finding himself at times still grieving over the death of his father some ten years after it occurred. He tells how he is often asked,

'When are you going to get over it?' Phillips replies: 'I'll get over my father's death at the resurrection and not one minute earlier!'[3] Finally, we need to remind ourselves that in ways we can never fully understand, God is sovereign in all matters of life and death. God knew how many days you would live on this earth even before you were born (Psalm 139:16)! Humbling yes, but also reassuring:

> Whate'er my God ordains is right:
> Here shall my stand be taken;
> Though sorrow, need or death be mine,
> Yet am I not forsaken.
> My Father's care
> Is round me there;
> He holds me that I shall not fall:
> And so to Him I leave it all.[4]

FOR FURTHER READING: LUKE 13:1–9

Reflect on these points:

1. 'The secret things belong to the LORD our God, but the things that are revealed belong to us and to our children forever' (Deut. 29:29).

2. Such events are meant to remind us that we all live under the shadow of death, reminding us of our own mortality.

3. God knew how many days you would live on this earth even before you were born.

An attitude
of gratitude

Chapter 22

Were there not ten cleansed? Where are the nine?
Was no one found to return and give praise to God
except this foreigner?

Luke 17:17–18

I guess airlines aren't very used to being thanked for exemplary service. Whilst flying west to east across the United States, I had to change planes in Chicago. Because my incoming flight was late I had hardly any time at all to transfer onto my next flight to Washington DC. I presumed that although I had made it onto the plane, there was little chance that my luggage had. So it was with no hope of success that I waited by the baggage carousel at Washington National Airport. But there were my bags! So I thought I'd just pop into the United Airlines office to thank them. As I approached the desk clerk, I was met with an order: 'Fill in a form!'

'But I just wanted to …'

'Fill in a form!'

'I just wanted to say …'

'Fill in a form!'

As the order got louder, I decided to leave. United never did get thanked! But then I wondered, sadly, how many happy, grateful passengers the desk clerk had ever encountered.

In the episode that Luke narrates here, Jesus had only a ten percent 'thank you' rate. It's quite a well-known gospel story, but we need to be careful to draw the right conclusions from it. Luke is not writing a guide to good manners. This is not a story he told us so that we'd say 'thank you' a bit more often. And then there's the puzzle at the end. What happened to the other nine? Did Jesus cancel their healing because of their ingratitude? And if we're meant to see healing from leprosy as a picture of salvation from sin—and we are—then, to put it bluntly, were the other nine saved?

This episode is set in the wilderness between Samaria and Galilee—the desolate geography accentuating the desolation of the lepers. According to old covenant law, such people were deprived of fellowship both with their fellow humankind and—because they were excluded from the temple—with God. Therefore, 'leprosy so well depicts the corrupting power and the condemning presence of sin'.[1] And that's why we are meant to see Jesus' healing people from leprosy as a picture of salvation from sin.

The story itself comes in three episodes. First, in verses 11–13, the lepers come to Jesus in the right way. They stand at a distance and plead for mercy. They know they have nothing to offer or to commend themselves. There would be no point waiting until their leprosy was healed before coming to Jesus! And for us, there's no point waiting until our sin is dealt with before coming to him. Indeed, theirs is a model of how we should pray: 'Jesus, Master, have mercy on us' (v. 13). It's the kind of prayer that God loves to answer.

It's the kind of prayer that Jesus commends and accepts— as we shall learn in Luke's next chapter in the prayer of the tax collector, 'God, be merciful to me, a sinner' (Luke 18:13).

Then secondly, in verse 14, we have a picture of salvation by grace, received through faith. First, there is Jesus' gracious response, telling them to 'go and show yourselves to the priests'. Notice there's no medicine, no washing, no touching—Jesus' words are sufficient. But what must they have thought? Surely the last people they wanted to see in their current condition were the priests who operated like public health inspectors. But then they believe his gracious words. And only as they obey does their healing become evident to them. 'And as they went, they were cleansed,' Luke tells us.

So far we have seen guilt and grace, and now thirdly we have gratitude as one of the lepers returns to praise and worship Jesus. Notice too, the detail that Luke includes that one who had 'lifted up his voice ... at a distance' moments earlier (v. 12) now 'praises with a loud voice ... at Jesus' feet' (v. 15). And of course it's significant that Luke identifies the grateful returnee as being a Samaritan, with the inference that the nine who did not return were Jews. It is a theme of the Gospels that the religious outsiders— Matthew the tax collector, the woman at Jacob's well, the penitent thief on the cross—more readily responded to the gospel than did the religious insiders. As John puts it: 'He came to his own, and his own people did not receive him' (John 1:11). And this is a stark warning if you're a church-going, even Bible-reading doer of good works. It's possible to be 'religious' but to remain completely untouched by the gospel of grace.

Thus we come to Jesus' threefold question which clearly expresses surprise. We read elsewhere that Jesus 'marvelled' at both faith (Luke 7:9) and at unbelief (Mark 6:6). And here he marvels at the ingratitude of the nine and the thankfulness of the one. But of the three questions Jesus asks, the most intriguing is the middle one—'Where are the nine?' And the most likely answer was that at that very moment they were en route to the temple to show themselves to the priests as healed lepers. After all, ungrateful though they were, they too had shown faith and Jesus tells the one returnee—as he tells countless others in the Gospels—'Your faith has made you well' (v. 19), not your gratitude. Undoubtedly the nine were healed from their leprosy, but were they saved from their sin? There are two schools of thought. To some commentators it seems they were not. 'Although these men were religious enough to know where to find a priest,' writes Philip Ryken, 'their hearts were not melted by the grace that God had shown to them in Christ. They were happy enough to be clean, but they did not see themselves as the recipients of undeserved mercy.'[2] Do you see God as some kind of cosmic butler—there only to deliver your wants? But to others this episode shows the ingratitude of those whom

Christ has saved. To Richard Phillips, therefore, it depicts 'how little gratitude wells up to Jesus Christ in the light of the enormity of what he has done' for the saved sinner.[3] We have been born again, clothed in the righteousness of Christ, given new and eternal life. And so these verses should spur in each true believer an attitude of gratitude for, as another commentator puts it: 'We increase the sweetness of God's gifts by our thankfulness for them.'[4] As the American evangelist Samuel Davies (1723–61) wrote in one of his hymns:

> O may this strange, this matchless love,
> This God-like miracle of grace—
> Teach mortal tongues, like those above,
> To raise this song of grateful praise!
> Who is a pardoning God like Thee?
> Or who has grace so rich and free?[5]

FOR FURTHER READING: LUKE 17:11–19

Reflect on these points:

1. *'Help meets them in the path of obedience' (J.C. Ryle). It's their 'going' that is the expression of their faith.*

2. *It's possible to be 'religious' but to remain completely untouched by the gospel of grace.*

3. *These verses should spur in each true believer an attitude of gratitude, for 'we increase the sweetness of God's gifts by our thankfulness for them' (Alexander Maclaren).*

Do you understand?

Chapter 23

Are you the teacher of Israel and yet you do not understand these things?

John 3:10

Many years ago, I was buying an apartment in Washington DC. One of the major struggles I faced was a difference in language and terminology. So, for example, what they called a first floor apartment we would call a ground floor apartment. And I dealt not with an estate agent but a realtor. But I especially remember one conversation with my realtor when she asked, 'Mr Bennett, do you want me to arrange lust insurance?' Well, what to say? Seeing my bafflement, she kindly explained that LUST is an acronym for Leaking Underground Storage Tank! The apartment block had an underground oil tank for the heating system and should it leak, as an owner, I would be partly liable. It would therefore be prudent to take out lust insurance in case of such an eventuality. Simple when you know!

In his conversation with Jesus, Nicodemus finds himself struggling to understand what Jesus is saying. He just doesn't understand the terminology! This was especially embarrassing because in his opening remarks to Jesus, this leading Pharisee sounded very confident of what he knew. 'Rabbi,' he says to Jesus, 'we know that you are a teacher come from God, for no one can do these signs that you do unless God is with him' (John 3:2). Nicodemus and his Pharisee friends claimed to 'know' that Jesus was just another teacher or prophet—like Moses, Samuel, Jonah or Elijah. Nicodemus thought he understood but he didn't. Those teachers and prophets were mere humans, but Jesus is God. They had come to teach about God, but Jesus is God and had come to reveal God to mankind.

One senses that Nicodemus is trying to flatter Jesus, and one also senses that there's a 'but' coming. But Jesus cuts him off in full flow by answering him, 'Truly, truly, I say to you, unless one is born again he cannot see the kingdom of God' (v. 3). And in that one sentence, Jesus sweeps away all that Nicodemus stands for and tells him the one thing he needs—to be remade by the power of God. And he does the same to you and to me. Whatever it is we're trusting in—morality, so-called good works, church membership, Christian homes—he says to each one of us: 'Unless one is born again, you cannot [even] see the kingdom of God.' He shatters our false, time-limited securities, so that he might offer us the only true, eternal security—new life in him.

The Greek word translated 'again' can also mean 'from above' but Nicodemus clearly takes it in the first meaning, hence his bafflement and his first two questions: 'How can a man be born when he is old? Can he enter a second time into his mother's womb and be born?' (v. 4). And these questions of themselves show the very truth that Jesus is trying to teach him—that without this spiritual rebirth, you cannot see or even understand the truths about God's kingly rule. But Jesus' answer will leave Nicodemus still baffled:

> Truly, truly, I say to you, unless one is born of water and the Spirit, he cannot enter the kingdom of God. That which is born of the flesh is flesh, and that which is born of the Spirit is spirit. Do not marvel that I said to you, 'You must be born again.' The wind blows where it wishes, and you hear its sound, but you do not know where it comes from or where it goes to. So it is with everyone who is born of the Spirit. (vv. 5–8)

So Nicodemus' third question gives voice to his continued bafflement. Water, wind, spirit—'How can these things be?' he asks Jesus (v. 9). But now it's time for Jesus to ask a question of Nicodemus: 'Are you the teacher of Israel and yet you do not understand these things?' (v. 10). And this question is the key for us to understand the conversation. Now, if Jesus were speaking of some entirely new doctrine, then Nicodemus' ignorance would be unsurprising. But Jesus is astounded that Nicodemus, 'the teacher of Israel' doesn't understand. One commentator writes:

> It was as if Jesus were saying, 'You don't know this? This is foundational biblical truth. This is not some mystery religion that I'm giving you ... I'm telling you something that any knowledgeable teacher of

the Old Testament should have grasped long ago. Why don't you, the teacher of Israel, understand these things?'[1]

So where in his Old Testament scrolls should teacher Nicodemus have been looking to put into context Jesus' reference to spiritual new birth, water, wind and spirit? And the answer is in the prophecy of Ezekiel where God proclaims through his prophet:

> I will sprinkle clean water on you, and you shall be clean from all your uncleanness, and from all your idols I will cleanse you. And I will give you a new heart, and a new spirit I will put within you. And I will remove the heart of stone from your flesh and give you a heart of flesh. And I will put my Spirit within you, and cause you to walk in my statutes and be careful to obey my rules.
>
> (Ezek. 36:25–27)

What follows on from these verses in Ezekiel is the vision of the valley of dry bones with its references to wind, breath and spirit (see chapter 10 of this volume). And, says Jesus, 'Nicodemus, you ought to know this, you Teacher of Israel. I've come to fulfil the Law and the Prophets. They point to me!' And so the man who began the conversation with the words 'we know' is shown to be utterly ignorant of spiritual things. Why? Because 'you must be born again', born from above. And it's the same for you and for me. We have to come to the point where we finally realise that in and of ourselves we can neither understand the gospel nor accomplish our own salvation. 'For God so loved the world, that he gave his only Son, that whoever believes in him should not perish but have eternal life' (John 3:16):

> O Breath of life, come sweeping through us,
> Revive Thy church with life and power;
> O Breath of life, come, cleanse, renew us,
> And fit Thy church to meet this hour.
>
> O Wind of God, come bend us, break us,
> Till humbly we confess our need;
> Then in Thy tenderness remake us,
> Revive, restore; for this we plead.[2]

FOR FURTHER READING: JOHN 3:1–21

Reflect on these points:

1. *Jesus shatters our false, time-limited securities, so that he might offer us the only true, eternal security—new life in him.*

2. *We have to come to the point where we finally realise that in and of ourselves we can neither understand the gospel nor accomplish our own salvation.*

Fickle followers

Chapter 24

Do you want to go away as well?

John 6:67

The British politician Chuka Umunna was elected as a Labour MP in 2010. In 2015, he stood as a candidate for leader of the Labour Party but lost to Jeremy Corbyn. On 18 February 2019, he—along with six other MPs—quit the Labour Party and formed a new party named Change UK. But following Change UK's dismal showing in the European elections in June of the same year, Umunna left Change UK and nine days later announced he was joining the Liberal Democrats! To Mr Umunna's critics, belonging to three different parties in four months showed him not as Mr Fearless but as Mr Fickle.

And some of the crowd who came to listen to Jesus' teaching appeared to be just as fickle. Having witnessed the feeding of the five thousand the day before, they commandeered boats to cross the Sea of Galilee in order to keep up with Jesus and hear his teaching. But a few verses later we read they were disenchanted with Jesus' teaching and head home. And it's that reaction that causes Jesus to pose this question to the Twelve: 'Do you want to go away as well?' (v. 67). All this raises two questions for us: Why did so many of the crowd so quickly turn against Jesus? How did the Twelve reply to Jesus' question?

John tells us 'that when many of his disciples heard [his teaching], they said, 'This is a hard saying; who can listen to it?' (v. 60). John did not mean 'hard to understand', but 'hard to accept'. Today, people will sometimes say, 'I can't understand', when the truth is they are really saying, 'I can't accept it'. Often apparent misunderstanding is a smoke screen for simply not wanting to submit to God's gospel call. Is that something you do?

So what was it that Jesus had been teaching about? In essence, two things. First, about his divine incarnation. He had spoken of his having 'come down from heaven' (vv. 33, 38, 51). And, like many today, the crowd refused to accept it (v. 42). Second, he talked about 'giving his flesh for the life of the world' (v. 51)—in other words 'the atonement made by his death, the satisfaction made by his sufferings, as our Substitute, the redemption effected by his enduring the penalty of our sins in his body on the tree'.[1] Jesus was talking about his earning salvation for us rather than us vainly trying to earn it for ourselves. And Boice rightly reminds us that 'nothing is more calculated to arouse the ire and rebellion of the human heart than this teaching' of salvation through God's grace rather than though our own merit.[2] That's why the crowds turned away, because Jesus' teachings ran counter to their way of thinking. People are often too proud to think they can't get salvation and heaven for themselves. So many of Jesus' disciples—his local followers, not the Twelve—'grumbled about this' (v. 61) and then they 'turned back and no longer walked with [Jesus]' (v. 66).

So observing this mass exodus of so-called disciples, Jesus turns to the Twelve and rather than congratulating them on staying around, he asks them, 'Do you want to go away as well?' (v. 67). 'Will you hear the Word of God, profess to believe it, but then turn your back on me and my teaching?' And he asks you and me the same question. Remember, Jesus was speaking to a group which numbered a mere twelve but it contained Judas Iscariot who would himself turn his back on him. So it is surely right to say that there will be many Judases within today's visible church. As Boice comments: 'There are some who profess to be Christians, who even hold office in Christian churches, but who have never been born again and who may one day openly turn their backs on all they stood for previously.'[3] What a warning to search our hearts and, before the all-seeing God, to ascertain that you can say with the apostle Paul, 'For I know whom I have believed...' (2 Tim. 1:12).

Now as we have seen in many previous chapters already, a number of Jesus' questions do not receive direct answers—but this one does. Verses 68–69: 'Simon Peter answered him, "Lord, to whom shall we go? You have the words of eternal life, and we have believed, and come to know, that you are the Holy One of God."' Jesus' relevant and highly searching question (v. 67) is met by an equally demanding and searching answer that speaks of staying with him both because of who he is and the paltry offers of the alternatives. So in verses 68–69, Simon Peter asks a question of his own on behalf of the Twelve.

There are three things that we need to see in this wonderfully profound answer. First, Peter had come to see the unsatisfying nature of the alternatives. 'To whom shall we go?' he asks rhetorically. And you? Would you be truly satisfied to return to your former way of life, or to secularism, atheism, or to false religions? Second, see that Peter, unlike those fickle followers who had already left, was attracted to Jesus not by his miracles but by his message. The same message that had proved unacceptable to them constitutes the very 'words of eternal life' to the true disciple. So I ask with all seriousness: What attracts you to Christ and his church? Is it the social life? Is it the music? Is it the ritual? Or is it because you have come to see the gospel—Christ's teaching—as that 'one pearl of great price' for which the person in Jesus' parable 'went and sold all that he had and bought it' (Matt. 13:46 NKJV).

Third, notice the order in which spiritual new birth occurs: 'We have believed,' says Peter, 'and have come to know, that you are the Holy One of God' (v. 69). A.W. Pink writes:

> It is the Divinely appointed and unchanging order in connection with spiritual things. Whoever heard

of believing in order to be sure? Man wants to make sure first before he is ready to believe. But God always reverses man's order of things. It is impossible to be sure of Divine truth until we have believed it.[4]

I pray that this conversation between our Lord and Peter will enable you to 'believe and come to know' that Jesus is indeed 'the Holy One of God' and so believing that you may persevere as a faithful follower:

> Thy works, not mine, O Christ,
> Speak gladness to this heart;
> They tell me all is done,
> They bid my fear depart.
> To whom save Thee, who canst alone
> For sin atone, Lord, shall I flee?[5]

FOR FURTHER READING: JOHN 6:41–71

Reflect on these points:

1. *Today, people will sometimes say, 'I can't understand', when the truth is 'I can't accept'.*

2. *'There are some who profess to be Christians but who have never been born again and who may one day openly turn their backs on all they stood for previously' (James Boice).*

3. *'It is impossible to be sure of Divine truth until we have believed it' (A.W. Pink).*

The most important question

Chapter 25

Do you believe in the Son of Man?

A book about questions in the Bible almost has to have a chapter dealing with John 9. For aficionados of questions, John 9 is a real treat for there are no fewer than seventeen questions posed during its forty-one verses. The Pharisees ask nine of them. Jesus asks just one—of the man born blind to whom he has just given his sight. But the question Jesus asks of him—'Do you believe in the Son of Man?'—is the big question. As one commentator rightly remarks: 'There is no more important question that can either be asked or answered.'[1]

John includes seven miracles in his Gospel, and this chapter tells the sixth, of Jesus healing a man born blind. And behind Jesus' giving sight to a man born blind, John wants us to see issues of spiritual sight and spiritual blindness. The fact that John devotes a whole chapter to this episode shows its importance. Briefly, the story thus far. Jesus had 'made mud with saliva ... anointed the man's eyes with the mud and said to him, "Go, wash in the pool of Siloam."' He obeyed 'and came back seeing' (John 9:6–7). But the Pharisees claim that Jesus, by making the mud, had profaned the Sabbath. So they interrogate both the newly-sighted man (vv. 13–17), and his parents (vv. 18–23) and then the man again (vv. 24–34). The parents don't want to get involved fearing they will be put out of the synagogue

(vv. 22–23), but the healed man becomes more bold in his answers to the Pharisees. Indeed, by the final exchange, he is teaching and admonishing them. To this, the Pharisees reply, 'You were born in utter sin, and would you teach us?' And they cast him out (v. 34).

We said earlier that this episode illustrates not only the sight of the blind but the blindness of the sighted. The man born blind receives his spiritual sight, but the Pharisees who see physically are shown to be spiritually blind. They serve as a grave warning. Again, we said at the start that during this chapter they ask nine questions! But all that illustrates is that it's possible to participate in religious debate without ever wanting to discover the truth about Jesus. In direct contrast to the blind man's spiritual journey towards the truth about Christ, the Pharisees remain trapped in their own prejudices, self-righteousness and self-importance. A man blind from birth has just received his sight and their response is to quibble over who made what on the Sabbath (v. 14)! Of Jesus they say: 'This man is not from God' (v. 16); 'we know that this man is a sinner' (v. 24). Like Nicodemus, their favourite phrase seems to be 'we know ... we know ...', not realising that spiritually they know nothing at all. If this is the way you talk about the Christian faith from outside of it, be warned.[2]

In direct contrast, John's narrative reveals how this once-blind man's understanding of Jesus slowly, but surely, deepens. At first, the man refers to Jesus as 'the man called Jesus' (v. 9). Then, in his first conversation with the Pharisees, he says that he thinks Jesus is 'a prophet' (v. 17) and by the end of the second conversation he says that Jesus must be 'from God' (v. 33). By this point, John wants us to realise the spiritual depth to the narrative. And it's to pursue this spiritual application of the story that John adds yet another seven verses to his chapter and that's where we pick up John's narrative, at verse 35. John tells us that 'Jesus heard that they had cast him out, and having found him, he said, "Do you believe in the Son of Man?"' The 'Son of Man' is the title that Jesus most frequently used for himself. It harks back to its use in a vision shown by God to Daniel in which the prophet was given the privilege of, as it were, looking into heaven. There he saw 'the Ancient of Days'—a reference to God the Father—taking his heavenly throne. Then he saw that 'there came one like a son of man, and he came to the Ancient of Days and was presented before him. And to him was given dominion and glory and a kingdom' (Dan. 7:13–14)—a reference to Jesus' ascension into heaven. So the title 'Son of Man' is not drawing attention to Jesus' humanity but to his divinity.[3] And Jesus is asking the man, 'Do you believe in this Son of Man?' Now clearly, the question was not a question like, 'Do you believe in Father Christmas?'—that is, do you believe he exists? Rather, by this question, Jesus was asking this man whether he put his whole trust and confidence in 'the Son of Man'—in the one who is God's revelation of himself to mankind. That's the big question! So what happens next?

In response, the man asks Jesus a question of his own: 'Who is he, sir, that I may believe in him?' (v. 36). Don Carson suggests that this question 'is probably not a request for information as to the Son of Man's characteristics and functions, but a request that the Son of Man be identified'.[4] And that's what Jesus immediately does. We read, 'Jesus said to him, "You have seen him, and it is he who is speaking to you"' (v. 37). It's worth remembering that up to the start of this conversation, the healed man had never seen Jesus.[5] But now he sees Jesus, not only physically but spiritually. 'Lord, I believe,' says the man to Jesus, and John records, 'he worshipped him' (v. 38)—the word means literally to kneel in homage. The man's journey of understanding is complete. Jesus was first 'the man', then 'a prophet', then 'from God', but now God! This is a double miracle, and the opening of the eyes of one born blind was the least of them! 'O happy man!' exclaims Ryle. 'Having lost the synagogue, he finds heaven!'[6] Have you done the same? Have you answered this most important of questions with true repentance and reverent worship? What this man discovered is that when you come to Jesus in that way, you will always be received and restored. As John Newton puts it:

Approach, my soul, the mercy-seat,
Where Jesus answers prayer;
There humbly fall before His feet,
For none can perish there.

Thy promise is my only plea,
With this I venture nigh:
Thou callest burdened souls to Thee,
And such, O Lord, am I.[7]

Have you come as a repentant sinner to this merciful Saviour and heard the same gracious reply as did this man? If not, Jesus' final comment to the Pharisees should be a stark warning: 'Your guilt remains!' (v. 41):

O wondrous love, to bleed and die,
To bear the cross and shame,
That guilty sinners such as I,
Might plead Thy gracious name.

FOR FURTHER READING: JOHN 9

Reflect on these points:
1. *It's possible to participate in religious debate without ever wanting to discover the truth about Jesus.*
2. *Have you answered this most important of questions with true repentance and reverent worship? What this man discovered is that when you come to Jesus in that way, you will always be received and restored.*

A matter of
life and death

Chapter 26

Do you believe this?

John 11:26

Many of us find the subject of death difficult. Many resort to euphemisms saying, for example, that someone has 'passed away'. I can remember when the Bennett family were out shopping in Derby—my father, mother, brother and I—when we met a near neighbour who was waiting outside the branch of a well-known pharmacy, what in those days we called a chemist. When my parents greeted her, she replied, 'I've just lost my husband', to which my father offered the instant—and in the circumstances highly inappropriate reply—'Well, I'm sure he'll turn up again very soon!' I don't quite remember how the conversation went from there but it was clear that what she had meant was that her husband had recently died!

Jesus was very fond of Mary, Martha and Lazarus—the sisters and brother of Bethany, just outside Jerusalem. So it's surprising to read that when Jesus heard that Lazarus was ill, 'he stayed two days longer in the place where he was' (John 11:6). Later, John records Jesus telling his disciples, 'Our friend Lazarus has fallen asleep, but I go to awaken him' (v. 11).[1] It's at this moment that the disciples make a similar mistake to that of my father, for they fail to realise that what Jesus really meant was 'Lazarus has died'

165

(v. 14). By the time Jesus arrived at Bethany, Lazarus had been dead four days (v. 17).

Hearing that Jesus is approaching, Martha goes out to meet him (v. 20). She opens her conversation with Jesus with the words which the anguished sisters had probably said dozens of times those last few days: 'Lord, if you had been here, my brother would not have died' (v. 21). It's easy to be critical of Martha here but it's not wrong for Christians to bring their thoughts frankly to the Lord. Read the Psalms, they're full of anguished cries of grief and complaint. A.W. Pink calls these words 'a strange mingling of faith and unbelief'.[2] How like us! But there are mistakes that Martha makes which we need to avoid. First, she limits Jesus' power by distance. She wrongly presumed that Jesus must be physically present in order to exercise his power. But Jesus healed the centurion's servant from afar (Matt. 8:13). Second, she presumes that it was Jesus' will that her brother should not die. And how often do we think that God has 'failed' us when something similar occurs to us? Be careful not to hold God to promises he never made.

And Jesus in his first reply (v. 23) gives what Don Carson calls 'a masterpiece of planned ambiguity'.[3] On one level he tells Martha that death is not the end, but on another level he is promising her brother's imminent resurrection. Of course, this is comfort that only Jesus can give, but it teaches us how to counsel a bereaved Christian believer—

do what Jesus did and point them to Jesus and his word. That's the best ministry that we can have to a bereaved brother or sister in Christ.

Martha sees Jesus' promise only on the first level. She, as it were, postpones Jesus' blessing until 'the last day' (v. 24). But Jesus has more for Martha—and for us—and now makes an even more wonderful announcement: 'I am the resurrection and the life' (v. 25). This is the fifth of the seven 'I am' statements that John records for us. And again, Jesus fixes Martha's thoughts on himself for 'it is not future events but the person of the Lord, ever present with us, that we need to be occupied with'.[4] As so often, Jesus tells us what we need and then tells us that he is what we need. In John 3:15, Jesus told Nicodemus that what he needed was eternal life and in the following verse that whoever believes in him shall 'have eternal life' (3:16). In John 4:10, Jesus told the Samaritan woman that what she needed was 'living water' and then announced that he was the very source of that living water (4:14). In John 6:32, Jesus told his disciples that what they needed was 'the bread from heaven' but that 'I am the bread of life' (6:35). Now, Jesus tells Martha that her brother needs resurrection and life, and that 'I am the resurrection and the life'. He not only gives living water, the bread of life, resurrection and life—he is those very things!

Jesus then elaborates on this by telling Martha: 'Whoever believes in me, though he die [physically], yet shall he live [eternally], and everyone who lives and believes in me shall never die'—literally, 'will never die for ever' (vv. 25–26). B.B. Warfield writes: 'Whatever Death is, and all that Death is ... that is what we shall be saved from in this salvation. And whatever Life is, and all that Life is ... that is what we shall be saved to in this salvation.'[5] But we need to notice that Jesus places a clear precondition on this when he prefaces this statement with the words, 'Whoever believes in me ...' (v. 25). And that gives us the immediate context of the question he now asks of Martha: 'Do you believe this?' (v. 26). And 'this' clearly refers to all that Jesus has said in these two verses.

I would suggest that John 11:27 is one of the hidden gems of the Bible. Most Bible students know of Peter's 'Great Confession' which seems to mark the turning point of the three synoptic Gospels. But here, hidden away in this most remarkable story, is a confession of similarly sublime revelation: 'Yes, Lord; I believe that you are the Christ, the Son of God, who is coming into the world.' Her opening two words—'Yes, Lord'—are the same two as we heard spoken by the two blind men when Jesus asked them, 'Do you believe that I am able to do this?' (Matt. 9:28). They are words of obedient faith. And then she carries Jesus' teaching further. She acknowledges her belief in Jesus as the Christ (that is, the Messiah and the Anointed One) and also in him being the Son of God— believing, therefore, that anyone who is the resurrection and the life can be so only by virtue of his deity. And her final acknowledgement of Jesus as the one 'who is coming into the world' proclaims Jesus as the fulfilment of the Old Testament prophecies all the way from Genesis 3:15, through Deuteronomy 18:18, 2 Samuel 7:16 and Isaiah 53.

Sadly no time remains to consider the grave-shattering events of the remainder of this chapter as Jesus shows himself to be truly 'the resurrection and the life'. But I must ask whether you can truly echo Martha's believing 'Yes, Lord'? For only if you can, and do, will you experience your own Easter Day:

> With holy joy, Lord Jesus, we sing the life you give,
> The hope you hold before us, the strength by which
> we live!
> Lead on in sovereign mercy through all life's
> troubled ways,
> Till resurrection bodies bring resurrection praise![6]

FOR FURTHER READING: JOHN 11:1–44

Reflect on these points:

1. *Be careful not to hold God to promises he never made.*

2. *As so often, Jesus tells us what we need and then tells us that he is what we need.*

3. *'Yes, Lord; I believe that you are the Christ, the Son of God, who is coming into the world.'*

Knowing
who Jesus is

Chapter 27

Have I been with you so long, and you still do not know me, Philip?

John 14:9

The noted actor, dramatist and humourist (and much else besides) Sir Peter Ustinov (1921–2004) loved telling the story of when he was once returning from a trip abroad at a time when he was something of a celebrity of stage and screen. He'd collected his luggage from the airport carousel but was stopped going through customs and told to open all his bags. Somewhat exasperated, he turned to the young customs officer and asked, 'Young man, do you know who I am?', to which the customs officer merely replied, 'No sir, I don't, but if you've forgotten, you'll find the name in your passport!' And in these verses we are looking at in John 14, it's as if Jesus turns to one of the Twelve, Philip, and says, 'Young man, don't you know who I am?' Needless to say, failing to recognise God is on an altogether higher plain than failing to recognise a film star!

At this point in his Gospel, John has completed his account of Jesus' public ministry (chapters 1–12) and now in chapters 13–17 he recounts Jesus' private teaching to the Twelve just before the events of the first Good Friday unfold. The section from 13:31–17:26 is often called 'The Farewell Discourse'. As we join the account, Jesus has just foretold both Judas' betrayal (13:21–30) and Peter's denial (13:36–38) as well as telling the disciples that he will soon be leaving them, and that 'where I am going you cannot come' (13:33). All that would doubtless have left the disciples distraught, and that's the context for the opening verse of chapter 14 where Jesus tells the disciples, 'Let not your hearts be troubled.' In the circumstances that may seem a rather odd thing for Jesus to say, but he goes on to give them—and us—good reason not to have troubled hearts. And that reason is that Christ has gone ahead to 'prepare a place for you' and that he 'will come again and will take you to myself, that where I am you may be also' (v. 3). Jesus is talking of each believer's place in heaven and of his Second Coming before adding, 'And you know the way to where I am going' (v. 4). As one hymn writer expresses it:

> Jesus lives, and reigns supreme;
> And, his kingdom still remaining,
> I shall also be with him,
> Ever living, ever reigning.
> God has promised; be it must:
> Jesus is my hope and trust.[1]

Thomas' comment (v. 5) means that, in effect, the Twelve still don't really understand who Jesus is or where he's going. So how, asks Thomas, can they know the way? Jesus replies with the sixth of the seven 'I am' statements recorded in John's Gospel: 'I am the way, and the truth, and the life. No one comes to the Father except through me' (v.

6). To careful readers of John's Gospel, this should come as no surprise. John has already told us that Jesus is 'the Word become flesh' (John 1:14), the 'Lamb of God, who takes away the sin of the world' (1:29), and 'the Saviour' (4:42). In Don Carson's words, Jesus is none other than 'God's gracious self-disclosure'.[2] So Jesus adds, 'If you had known me, you would have known my Father also. From now on you do know him and have seen him' (v. 7).[3]

It strikes me that Jesus is using the same teaching technique here that he used in his conversation with Martha—that 'masterpiece of planned ambiguity' that we mentioned in the previous exposition. It's almost as if Jesus' statement in verse 7 is given in order to prompt a question and develop the discussion—just as he did with Martha—and Philip takes the bait. 'Lord, show us the Father, and it is enough for us' (v. 8), says Philip. Don't you sometimes have similar thoughts? Maybe Philip was thinking of those Old Testament figures, Moses and Elijah, who were granted an extraordinary glimpse of the glory of God, but even they didn't actually see God as he is himself. As God explained to Moses: 'You cannot see my face, for man shall not see me and live' (Exod. 33:20). But maybe Philip would settle for a theophany, and that's probably what Philip had in mind when he asked Jesus to 'show us the father'.

That's what brings about Jesus' question specifically to Philip and—as Philip had talked about showing 'us'—by implication to all the Twelve, and also to us. It's really two questions separated by a statement: 'Have I been with you so long, and you still do not know me, Philip? Whoever has seen me has seen the Father. How can you say, "Show us the Father?"' (v. 9). Philip hadn't yet realised that a 'show us the Father' moment was quite unnecessary because, 'a far more glorious revelation of Deity was there right before him'.[4] He was looking at the very one of whom John had earlier written: 'The Word became flesh and dwelt among us, and we have seen his glory, glory as of the only Son from the Father, full of grace and truth' (John 1:14). He was being addressed by the one of whom the apostle Paul would write, 'He is the image of the invisible God' (Col. 1:15), and that 'in him dwells all the fullness of the Godhead bodily' (Col. 2:9 NKJV).

So far, the discussion had centred on 'knowing' and 'seeing'. Between verses 4 and 9, the words 'know' or 'known' appear seven times; the words 'see' or 'show' appear four times. But as Jesus continues the conversation in verses 10–14, none of these words appear again. Jesus turns the conversation from 'seeing' and 'knowing' to 'believing':

- 'Do you not believe … ?' (v. 10)
- 'Believe me that I am in the Father and the Father is in me or else, believe on account of the works themselves' (v. 11)
- 'Whoever believes in me …' (v. 12)

In most areas of life, we tend to say that 'seeing is believing'. But it's an oft-repeated principle of the gospel that 'believing is seeing'. Only once we believe do we truly see. As Jesus explained to Martha just before he raised her brother from the grave: 'Did I not tell you that if you believed you would see the glory of God?' (John 11:40). So in closing, I must ask: 'Do you believe these great truths about the Lord Jesus Christ?' Do you as a result see clearly who Jesus is? As Martha put it: 'Yes, Lord; I believe that you are the Christ, the Son of God, who is coming into the world' (John 11:27).

FOR FURTHER READING: JOHN 14:1–14

Reflect on these points:

1. *Jesus is none other than 'God's gracious self-disclosure' (Don Carson).*

2. *Philip hadn't yet realised that a 'show us the Father' moment was quite unnecessary because, 'a far more glorious revelation of Deity was there right before him' (A.W. Pink).*

3. *In most areas of life, we tend to say that 'seeing is believing'. But it's an oft-repeated principle of the gospel that 'believing is seeing'. Only once we believe do we truly see.*

The Son asks
the Father

Chapter 28

My God, my God, why have you forsaken me?

Matthew 27:46

We return to Matthew's Gospel as we consider, finally, four questions that are asked just before or following Jesus' crucifixion and resurrection. The Gospels record seven statements made by Jesus from the cross, often referred to (somewhat misleadingly) as Jesus' 'last words'. Matthew and Mark alone record this particular statement in which Jesus directs a question to God the Father by quoting the opening words of Psalm 22, 'My God, my God, why have you forsaken me?' Of all the thirty-one questions we have chosen to consider in this book, this one is unique in the sense that it is the only one in which the question is asked by and of a person of the Divine Trinity—being asked by God the Son of God the Father.

The immediate context of the question is also of the utmost importance. In the verse preceding our lead text, Matthew records: 'Now from the sixth hour there was darkness over all the land until the ninth hour' (Matt. 27:45)—that's between noon and three in the afternoon. As one commentator puts it: 'The link between the darkness and the cry is very close: the first is a symbol of the agonising content of the second.'[1] Luke records that 'the sun's light failed' (Luke 23:45) and it is correct to regard this as one of the miracles of this awesome day. Biblically, darkness is often used as a metaphor for judgement both in the prophetic writings of the Old Testament and in Jesus' teaching.[2] All four Gospels are silent on what occurred during these three dark hours.

Matthew then records (27:46) that at 'about the ninth hour Jesus cried out with a loud voice, saying, "Eli, Eli lema sabachthani?" that is, "My God, my God, why have you forsaken me?"' This is the only recorded prayer of Jesus with the address being to 'my God' rather than to 'my Father'. This heightens the sense of abandonment—of Jesus being cut off from God the Father. But as with all the questions that God—or Jesus—asks, Jesus well knew the answer to his question. As John White explains:

> Jesus knew the answer to his own agonised cry. He knew why. He had known during his earthly ministry. He had known with awful clarity in the Mount of Olives. His question was not a plea for intellectual understanding but an expression of agony that overwhelmed understanding.[3]

Jesus knew the prophecies of God's Suffering Servant that he would fulfil in order to accomplish God's eternal plan of salvation. He had just talked the night before of 'having accomplished the work that you [God the Father] gave me to do' (John 17:4). And as Jesus steps towards the arresting party in Gethsemane, John further records:

'Jesus, knowing all that would happen to him, came forward' (John 18:4). Jesus knew. He always does.

But let us try to grasp the full significance of these wondrous events by asking three questions. So first, what was occurring at this most awful moment? Just the night before these events Jesus had told his disciples that although they would all desert him, 'and will leave me alone, yet I am not alone, for the Father is with me' (John 16:32). Yet now, on the cross, in the darkness, he is utterly alone. That is why we do well to focus not so much on Jesus' physical suffering on the cross—though that was awful enough—but on his spiritual suffering.

So now we ask, for whom did Christ die? The apostle Paul answers that question: 'Christ died for the ungodly ... in that while we were still sinners, Christ died for us' (Rom. 5:6, 8). Christ's death was a real atonement for the specific sins of all those who would come to saving faith in him. Christ died as a substitute—in your place, in my place. When the famous theologian Karl Barth was asked what he thought was the most important word in the Bible, he replied that it was the Greek word 'hyper' that means 'for', 'on behalf of', 'in the place of'—that Jesus became sin 'for us', that he became a curse 'for us'.[4] This is what in Christian theology we call substitutionary atonement. That's what the prophecy of God's Suffering Servant is all about in Isaiah 53. So at Calvary, Jesus was cut off from his Father by your sin and mine, so that such a fate would not be ours. He was paying the price, the debt, of that sin so that both the wrath of God against you for your sin might be turned aside, and yet at the same time the justice of God might be satisfied. Elizabeth Clephane (1830–69) expresses it with clarity and beauty when she writes of Calvary:

O safe and happy shelter!
O refuge tried and sweet!
O trysting-place where heaven's love
And heaven's justice meet![5]

God's amazing love was shown and God's awful justice was satisfied at the cross of Christ.

Finally, what was achieved at Calvary? Theologically this is the very crossroads of our salvation, because this is the moment when, as the apostle Paul puts it, God 'made [Jesus] who knew no sin to be sin for us' (2 Cor. 5:21 NKJV), and when 'Christ redeemed us from the curse of the law by becoming a curse for us' (Gal. 3:13). Everything that Christ wins for us was won by his blood at Calvary. The New Testament writers tell us that as a result of Christ's blood shed on the cross we have been justified (Rom. 5:9), cleansed from sin (1 John 1:7) and the record and debt of our past sins cancelled (Col. 2:14); we have been redeemed (Eph. 1:7), ransomed (1 Peter 1:18–19), brought near to God (Eph. 2:13), reconciled to God (Col. 1:20, 22) and given access to God (Heb. 10:29); God's righteous anger towards our sin has been propitiated (Rom. 3:25);

we are clothed in Christ's righteousness (Rev. 7:14); Satan is defeated (Rev. 12:10–11) and Jesus is crowned with glory (Heb. 2:9)!

May this anguished cry of the Saviour cause you to seek your sole refuge in him, and then stir up in your heart both a true hatred of the sin which was the cause of his suffering and everlasting thankfulness for the amazing love he has shown to you:

> My sin,—O the bliss of this glorious thought!—
> My sin, not in part, but the whole,
> Is nailed to his cross, and I bear it no more;
> Praise the Lord, praise the Lord, O my soul.[6]

FOR FURTHER READING: ISAIAH 53:1–6; MATTHEW 27:32–54

Reflect on these points:

1. *'Jesus expressed this horror of great darkness, this God-forsakenness, by quoting the only verse of Scripture which accurately described it, and which he had perfectly fulfilled' (John Stott).*

2. *God's amazing love was shown and God's awful justice was satisfied at the cross of Christ.*

3. *'For He made Him who knew no sin to be sin for us, that we might become the righteousness of God in Him' (2 Cor. 5:21 NKJV).*

The suffering
Saviour

Was it not necessary that the Christ should suffer these things and enter into his glory?

Luke 24:26

If one were to make a film of the final chapter of Luke's Gospel, my guess is that you wouldn't be quite sure whether to call it a comedy or a tragedy. As Luke penned these verses, he must have surely had a chuckle. As Hugh Palmer remarks, 'If this were a pantomime, the audience would be shouting, "He's beside you!"'[1] Luke certainly didn't spare Cleopas' blushes by recording for posterity that he was the character who asked Jesus, 'Are you the only visitor to Jerusalem who does not know the things that have happened there in these days?' (v. 18). The irony was, of course, that it was Cleopas who didn't know what had happened, not Jesus. It reminds one of being in the situation where you have the last few pieces to fit into the jigsaw to complete the picture, but you still can't do it. Yes, you have all the pieces, but you just can't put them in their right place.

And these two had quite a lot of the jigsaw sorted. They knew Jesus was 'a man who was a prophet mighty in deed and word before God and all the people' (v. 19). They knew that it was Jewish religious leaders who had been behind getting Jesus condemned to death (v. 20). They had even remembered that 'the third day' had a significance (v. 21), though they couldn't bring themselves to believe 'some women' who found an empty tomb and had an angel tell them that 'he was alive' (vv. 22–23). As one commentator writes of Cleopas and his companion: 'In this confession … one clearly sees the violent struggle between hope and fear that raged in their hearts.'[2] As a result, they had a creed without a resurrection, and as the former Anglican Archbishop Michael Ramsey remarked, 'The gospel without the resurrection is not merely a gospel without its final chapter, it is not a gospel at all.'[3]

Where they go wrong is in verse 21: 'But we had hoped …' Like so many people today, they want to squeeze Jesus into their mould, their expectations and needs. When they said they 'had hoped that he was the one to redeem Israel', it seems clear that they were thinking of freedom from the Romans, not from sin. Their hopes were entirely this-worldly not other-worldly. Their creed had no room for a Suffering Saviour or for a resurrected Messiah. That's why Jesus' arrest, crucifixion and death had brought them nothing but sadness and despair (v. 17). They failed to see that it was precisely these events which were among the many authenticating signs that Jesus was indeed the promised Messiah.

Once Cleopas has given his breathless account of the 'things that had happened'—he barely pauses for breath for six verses (vv. 19–24)—Jesus gives a rebuke. 'O foolish ones, and slow of heart to believe all that the prophets have spoken,' Jesus admonishes them. And then he poses his question: 'Was it not necessary that the Christ should suffer these things and enter into his glory?' (v. 26). Do you see, Jesus goes straight to the very point over which they had stumbled—'that the Christ should suffer'. And then, doubtless to the great wonder and amazement of these two disciples, Jesus proceeded to answer the question for them, 'beginning with Moses and all the Prophets, he interpreted to them in all the Scriptures the things concerning himself' (v. 27)—as one commentator puts it so beautifully, 'The Word of God Incarnate explained the Word of God written!'[4]

Between verse 27 and verse 28 is one of the great silences of Scripture! On most occasions, conjecture where God is silent is unprofitable. But this just might be the exception. After all, it's just as important that we understand where we find Christ in the Old Testament as it was for these two disciples. Now some of my readers may be a little nervous of this approach to biblical interpretation. Maybe you had an unhelpful experience with people who 'saw Jesus behind every bush (burning or otherwise) in the Old Testament'.[5] But Jesus here sets us a clear example which we need to follow. So, where to look?

First, we can see promises God made in the Old Testament that Jesus clearly fulfils:

- The Seed (offspring) of the woman that would 'bruise Satan's head' (Gen. 3:15)

- That in Abraham 'all the families of the earth shall be blessed' (Gen. 12:3)
- To David that 'your throne shall be established for ever' (2 Sam. 7:16)[6]

And then there were the prophecies that Jesus fulfilled, for example of:

- Immanuel, born of a virgin (Isa. 7:14)
- A child-son to be born whose name shall be called 'Wonderful Counsellor, Mighty God, Everlasting Father, Prince of Peace' (Isa. 9:6)
- The Suffering Servant (Isa. 53)

And for these two disciples, the last prophecy would have been especially significant for it would show them how, as Jesus put it, 'the Christ should suffer these things'.

But we should also look to the types and figures of the Old Testament that point forward to their fulfilment in Jesus. The whole ritual of the Passover in Exodus 12—with the innocent, spotless lamb whose blood protects from the destroying angel—points to Christ, 'the Lamb of God'. The whole exodus narrative, also in Exodus 12, through which God's people are rescued from the slavery of Egypt is a type, a signpost, to the deliverance that Christ wins for his people through the cross rescuing them from slavery to sin. The scapegoat, which figuratively bore the sin of the people on the Day of Atonement in Leviticus 16, points to Christ. The bronze serpent, lifted up at God's command in Numbers 21 before the children of Israel so that whoever looked to it lived, points to Christ. Christ is the great High Priest, he is the new temple, he is the bread from heaven.

Back in Luke 24, we're told that the eyes of these two 'were kept from recognising [Jesus]' (v. 16), presumably by a direct act of God. It was only after he went into their home and shared a meal with them that as he 'took the bread and blessed and broke it and gave it to them, their eyes were opened, and they recognised him' (vv. 30–31). That was the moment of recognition, but what did they say? 'Did not our hearts burn within us while ... he opened to us the Scriptures?' (v. 32). We ignore Scripture at our peril:

> Lord, grant that we aright may learn
> The wisdom it imparts,
> And to its heavenly teaching turn
> With simple, childlike hearts.[7]

FOR FURTHER READING: LUKE 24:13–35

Reflect on these points:

1. 'The gospel without the Resurrection is not merely a gospel without its final chapter, it is not a gospel at all.' (Michael Ramsey)

2. 'Was it not necessary that the Christ should suffer these things and enter into his glory?'

3. In the Old Testament we will find God's plan of salvation through Christ signposted along the way.

Come and
have breakfast

Chapter 30

Children, do you have any fish?

John 21:5

Breakfast is my favourite meal. So John 21:12 is a verse that I'm naturally drawn to: 'Jesus said to them, "Come and have breakfast."' And for our final two expositions, we're in the last chapter of John's Gospel considering, first, Jesus' before-breakfast question, and then his after-breakfast questions. And here is important theology, practical application and touches of eye-witness authenticity. We discover more about Jesus' post-resurrection appearances, the importance of doing things at Christ's command, the vastness of the gospel's reach, and of Jesus' graciousness and care for his children.

This episode is bookended with the statement that Jesus 'revealed' himself again to the disciples (vv. 1, 14). That's how his post-resurrection appearances tended to occur. Suddenly, he's just there, in the garden, on the Emmaus Road, in the locked room and now here on the shore of the Sea of Galilee. We do need to remember that when we talk of the risen body of Jesus, we're talking of a great mystery. On the one hand, it's a very normal body. He talks, he walks, he's touchable, he has flesh and bones, he eats, he even cooks. But on the other hand, it's a transformed body, what David Turner calls 'humanity plus'.[1] He's no longer bound by material or spatial limitations. He can pass through a sealed tomb and through locked doors.

Well, after the roller-coaster of the previous days, seven of the disciples are on the lakeside and Peter announces, 'I am going fishing' (v. 3). One commentator remarks that 'never has a fishing trip been so severely judged!'[2] But there is no indication in the text that by doing so they were doing anything sinful. And, after all, they do still need to eat. We know that at least three of the seven were experienced fishermen who knew the lake well, 'but that night they caught nothing' (v. 3). Then 'just as day was breaking' (v. 4), Jesus 'revealed himself' about 100 yards away on the shore. But again, the disciples do not recognise him. 'Children, do you have any fish?' he asks. As always, the divine question is not seeking information but getting those to whom the question is addressed to face the situation they're in. Their answer—'No'—is followed this time by a command of Jesus, to 'cast the net on the right side of the boat and you will find some' (v. 6). First, there's a mini-miracle. They obey! As Bruce Milne dryly observes: 'Experienced fishermen are not noted for their ready appreciation of the advice of strangers, particularly one still on land.'[3] If they had already recognised Jesus, then their obedience would have made more sense. But they obey.

Then there's a major miracle as their net is overwhelmed by a veritable tsunami of fish—153 to be exact (v. 11). Throughout his Gospel, John loves to point us to Jesus' miracles referring to them as 'signs'. We looked at two of them in previous chapters. John doesn't use the word 'sign' here but it's undoubtedly a miracle. And just as with Jesus' miracles of giving sight to a man born blind and of raising Lazarus from the grave, we're meant to see the spiritual significance behind it. This is a sign that looks back and forward. It must have reminded these disciples of an occasion some three years earlier when Jesus had performed a similar miracle as he commissioned them as disciples. 'From now on,' he had told them, 'you will be catching men' (Luke 5:10). So it's as if Jesus is re-commissioning them for the Great Commission that is but a few weeks away—and then Pentecost.

And looking forward, Jesus wants them—and us—to see that his earlier teaching, that 'apart from me you can do nothing' (John 15:5), is true. Oh yes, they knew all about fishing. But they still caught nothing until they adopted the God-given strategy. And in today's church, it's tempting to rely on the strategies, the 'right' evangelism courses, or whatever, and prayer and God's power get relegated down our list of priorities. Jesus says to us: 'Apart from me you can do nothing.' He wants us to see what Richard Phillips calls 'the futility of labouring [for the gospel] according to our own wisdom', or to put that in the positive, that 'those who labour in obedience to Christ's Word will enjoy Christ's provision'.[4]

Many bottles of ink have been spilt trying to discern the spiritual symbolism of the number 153! But as Don

Carson wisely remarks: 'If the Evangelist has some symbolism in mind connected with the number 153, he has hidden it well!'[5] I think we're meant to draw no more from the number than its size—and after all, do you know a fisherman who doesn't count his catch? But in that size, there is a sign—a sign of the spiritual harvest which the disciples were about to witness. Turn but a couple of pages in your Bible to read that following Peter's Pentecost sermon 'those who received his word were baptised, and there were added that day about three thousand souls' (Acts 2:41).

But back to John's narrative. It was seeing the great quantity of fish and the way they had caught them that leads to the disciples' recognition of the stranger on the shore. John—'that disciple whom Jesus loved' (v. 7)—and Peter respond just as they did days earlier at the empty tomb. John exhibits the quick insight: 'It is the Lord.' Peter exhibits the quick action, diving into the water and swimming to the shore where Jesus awaits them complete with charcoal fire, fish and bread (v. 9). Wouldn't you just love to know how those bits and pieces got there? But on such subjects John is silent, for he wants to tell us about the graciousness of the Saviour to his children. 'Bring some of the fish that *you* have just caught,' Jesus says to the disciples. 'That *you* have just caught?' Isn't that truly gracious? Jesus gives us so much and then counts it as ours to offer back to him! And what do seven weary fishermen most need after a long night out on the water but a hearty meal?

And even when, maybe like these seven disciples, we're just a bit reluctant to come to Jesus, he issues the specific and personal and unmistakable invitation which in this instance was 'Come and have breakfast!':

> I heard the voice of Jesus say,
> 'Come unto me and rest;
> Lay down, thou weary one, lay down
> Thy head upon my breast.'
> I came to Jesus as I was,
> Weary and worn and sad,
> I found in Him a resting-place,
> And He has made me glad.[6]

FOR FURTHER READING: JOHN 21:1–14

Reflect on these points:

1. *In his resurrection, Christ is the 'firstfruits' of the new creation—'Christ the firstfruits, then at his coming those who belong to Christ' (1 Cor. 15:23).*

2. *Jesus wants us to see 'the futility of labouring [for the gospel] according to our own wisdom' (Richard Phillips).*

3. *Jesus gives us so much and then counts it as ours to offer back to him!*

Re~comissioned

Chapter 31

Do you love me more than these?

John 21:15

The fish had been (miraculously) caught, breakfast cooked and consumed, now it was time for the conversation—between Jesus and Peter, the disciple who had just days, earlier, denied his Lord three times. And we really do need to see Jesus' questioning of Peter in the context of these previous events. For it was not only the denial of which Peter had been guilty, but of boastful self-confidence. When Jesus had spoken of going away and that the disciples would not be able to follow him, Peter was so quick to say: 'Lord, why can I not follow you now? I will lay down my life for you' (John 13:37)—notice, not 'we' but 'I'. Indeed Matthew records Peter making a direct comparison with the other disciples: 'Though they all fall away because of you, I will never fall away' (Matt. 26:33). So Peter was on the record as thinking he was stronger, better, more devoted to Jesus than the others. How Peter must have brooded over those public boasts in the days after the crucifixion. The tears that he shed even in the high priest's courtyard immediately after the dreadful event were tears of remorse. And now Jesus was alive again, what would he say? Well after breakfast, Peter was to find out.

One wonders what Peter made of the scene he found as he swam ashore from the fish-laden boat (vv. 7–9). There was Jesus—the one whom he had denied whilst warming himself at 'a charcoal fire' in the high priest's courtyard (John 18:18)—on the shore with 'a charcoal fire' in place (John 21:9)! A.W. Pink suggests: 'How this fire by the sea would prick Peter's conscience: a silent preacher, but a powerful one.'[1] And in the conversation that followed we have a searching question, a humble response and a gracious command.

How merciful is Jesus as he begins the conversation, not with reproach, or condemnation, but with a question about love. But how carefully is this searching question crafted for it invites Peter to—yet again—compare his love for Jesus with the love that the others had for Jesus, not just, 'Do you love me?' but 'Do you love me more than these?' And, significantly, Jesus asks it three times, though the second and third times without the comparative twist at the end. We know that the significance of the asking three times was not lost on Peter for we read that on the third time of asking 'Peter was grieved' (v. 17).[2]

But the searching question brings forth a humble response. Gone now is the boastful self-confidence—the 'I'm better than everyone else'. The courtyard denial of his Master was a turning point in Peter's life. The boastful days were gone. Though asked to rate his love for Jesus against that of the other disciples, Peter does not do so but is content to make a humble, 'Yes, Lord', before appealing to the Lord's better knowledge—'You know that

I love you.' Here are echoes of Ezekiel's faithful response to God's question concerning the possibility of life in the dry bones: 'O LORD God, you know' (Ezek. 37:3). Of all the answers given to questions that God asks, this is perhaps the most humble and the most faithful.

But we need to notice Peter's being 'grieved' (v. 17) when the question is asked a third time. We should be grieved at the memory of our sin, for only when we see the loathsomeness of sin will we see clearly our need of a Saviour. Today's trend in many churches to 'tone down' the wording of any public confession of sin—to merely 'saying sorry' as if we had inadvertently knocked into someone in the street—is unbiblical and should be resisted.

So we've seen a searching question, a humble response, and now finally a gracious command as Jesus says to Peter, 'Feed my lambs' (v. 15), repeating it twice with minor variations (vv. 16, 17). Notice that Christian ministry is described in verbs not nouns.[3] Tending Christ's flock is something neither mystical nor monastic. It's highly practical. And Jesus commands Peter to 'feed' and 'tend' his flock, not be a pastor, minister or any other similar title. I'm not suggesting that one shouldn't be a pastor or minister—or whatever, hopefully biblical, title your church uses—but the title isn't what's important. It's the task. Jesus had already commissioned Peter as an evangelist when, some three years earlier, by the same lake, he had, with reference to Peter's previous trade as a fisherman, told him that 'from now on you will be catching men' (Luke 5:10).[4] And now Jesus resorts to the well-used biblical metaphor of the shepherd tending and feeding the sheep to re-commission Peter as a pastor. Peter fulfilled this new commission and passed it on. Here he is writing some thirty years later to scattered Jewish Christians:

> So I exhort the elders among you ... shepherd the flock of God that is among you, exercising oversight, not under compulsion, but willingly, as God would have you; not for shameful gain, but eagerly; not domineering over those in your charge, but being examples to the flock. And when the chief Shepherd appears, you will receive the unfading crown of glory.
>
> (1 Pet. 5:1-4)

Just as Peter is commissioned as a pastor to Christ's flock, so he commissions you and me to tend and feed his sheep. We may not have that as our title within the church, but we each have that role to play as we care for those who are his. As one commentator reminds us: 'Genuine New Testament conversion means not only turning to and accepting Christ. It also means turning to and accepting his bride, the church.'[5]

As we close these thirty-one expositions, having been reminded of so many of the wondrous ways in which God has, and continues to, show his love to penitent sinners, here is a hymn you can use to offer your response to the God, to the Saviour, who asks us as he asked Peter, 'Do you love me?':

> My Jesus, I love You, I know You are mine;
> For You all the pleasures of sin I resign:
> To You, my Redeemer and Saviour, I bow –
> If ever I loved You, my Jesus, 'tis now.
>
> My Jesus, I love You, for You first loved me,
> And purchased my pardon on Calvary's tree;
> I love You for wearing the thorns on Your brow,
> If ever I loved You, my Jesus, 'tis now.[6]

FOR FURTHER READING: JOHN 21:15–25

Reflect on these points:

1. *We should be grieved at the memory of our sin, for only when we see the loathsomeness of sin will we see clearly our need of a Saviour.*

2. *'Genuine New Testament conversion means not only turning to and accepting Christ. It also means turning to and accepting his bride, the church' (Bruce Milne).*

Questions God asks

Epilogue

Maybe you had never noticed before how much God, in the Old Testament, and Jesus, in the New Testament, like to ask questions. Having spent a lifetime in teaching, I soon came to realise that asking questions is one of the best teaching techniques, especially when through your questioning you enable a student either to see issues they'd never seen before or to understand things that, until then, were unclear. Writing on Jesus' question to Martha in John 11:26—'Do you believe this?'—A.W. Pink states: 'Every Divine communication challenges the heart to which it is made.'[1] And so as you read these thirty-one selected verses, your response is called for.

True, a number of the questions we studied were asked rhetorically, the answer being implied by the context. So God wasn't expecting a spoken answer when he asked Abraham, 'Is anything to hard for the LORD?' (Gen. 18:14), or when he asked, through Isaiah, 'To whom then will you compare me, that I should be like him?' (Isaiah 40:25). The answers—'no' and 'no one'—are clearly implied. Similarly, when Jesus asked the Pharisees and teachers of the law, 'Which is easier to say, "Your sins are forgiven," or to say, "Rise and walk"?' (Luke 5:23), no spoken answer was expected and none is recorded. But even the rhetorical questions demand an answer in the heart of you, the reader.

Indeed, it's interesting to ponder for a moment those answers that are recorded in Scripture. Of the thirty-one questions we considered, answers by the person to whom they were addressed are recorded on thirteen occasions. But what a variety they are! Cain tells a bare-faced lie when asked by God, 'Where is Abel your brother?' (Gen. 4:9), saying 'I do not know', before throwing a question back at his divine questioner, 'Am I my brother's keeper?' And maybe sometimes we are tempted to try and reverse the roles and address God as if he is answerable to us. But as the apostle Paul reminds us: 'But who are you, O man, to answer back to God? Will what is moulded say to its moulder, "Why have you made me like this?"' (Rom. 9:20). As Philip Ryken wisely teaches us: 'If there is going to be an interrogation, God is going to ask the questions. We do not question God. God questions us. We do not place God under our microscope. God places us under his.'[2]

At least one of Jesus' questions is answered correctly but one suspects grudgingly. After Jesus has told the parable of the moneylender forgiving the two debtors—one is forgiven 500 denarii and the other fifty—Jesus asks Simon the Pharisee, 'Now which of them will love him more?' Luke records Simon's reply as, 'The one, I suppose, for whom he cancelled the larger debt' (Luke 7:42–43). It's as if Simon is saying, 'Well, okay, I suppose you're right! You win!' But he has no understanding at all of the implication of his 'correct' answer. He still doesn't really get Jesus' teaching about forgiveness and grace for sinners. And the lawyer's answer to Jesus' question about the parable of the Good Samaritan (Luke 10:37) could well fall into the same category.

But there are also some wonderfully faithful answers given by, for example, Isaiah (6:8), Ezekiel (37:3), the two blind men (Matt. 9:28), Martha (John 11:27) and Peter (John 21:15–17) all of whom exhibit in their responses a faithful, trusting and willing heart. Indeed, both Ezekiel and Peter acknowledge in their answers the superior knowledge of God. When asked by God, 'Can these bones live?' Ezekiel replies, 'O LORD God, you know.' When asked by Jesus, 'Do you love me?' Peter replies, 'Lord you know everything.' There's an example to follow.

These thirty-one questions that God asks show the remarkable way in which the Bible is indeed 'A Book for All Seasons'. So hear God speaking to you through the pages of his holy, inerrant and life-giving word. Maybe you wouldn't yet call yourself a Christian, and you hear Jesus ask you, 'Who do you say that I am?' (Matt. 16:15); 'Do you believe in the Son of Man?' (John 9:35). What will you answer? Or maybe, you have called yourself a Christian all your life, but it makes not the slightest difference to the way to live your life. And now you hear Jesus ask you, 'Why do you call me, "Lord, Lord," and not do what I tell you?' (Luke 6:46). How will you answer? Or perhaps you're a Christian weighed down with the burdens of life, struggling with loneliness, illness, bereavement, and God comes to you and tenderly asks you, 'Is anything to hard for the LORD?' (Gen. 18:14); 'Why are you afraid, O you of little of faith?' (Luke 8:25).

Someone who struggled with life and with his faith was William Cowper (1731–1800). Yet he left us a wondrous legacy of scriptural hymns that have been a blessing and a solace to generations of believers. In one of his best-loved hymns, Cowper imagines a conversation between the believer and his Saviour. During this poetic conversation the Saviour, as it were, reminds the believer of many of the wonderful things he has done for every forgiven sinner, of some of his most reassuring attributes and all interspersed with a number of questions, which, in the final verse of the hymn, the believer answers. In closing, may I commend this hymn to you in order that you too might have that same conversation and respond in faith and love to your Saviour's questions:

> Hark, my soul, it is the Lord!
> 'Tis thy Saviour, hear His word;
> Jesus speaks, and speaks to thee:
> 'Say, poor sinner, lov'st thou Me?
>
> 'I delivered thee when bound,
> And when bleeding, healed thy wound;
> Sought thee wandering, set thee right,
> Turned thy darkness into light.

'Can a woman's tender care
Cease towards the child she bare?
Yes, she may forgetful be,
Yet will I remember thee.

'Mine is an unchanging love,
Higher than the heights above,
Deeper than the depths beneath,
Free and faithful, strong as death.

'Thou shalt see My glory soon,
When the work of grace is done:
Partner of My throne shalt be;
Say, poor sinner, lov'st thou Me?'

Lord, it is my chief complaint
That my love is weak and faint:
Yet I love Thee and adore;
O for grace to love Thee more![3]

Amen. To God alone be glory!

Questions God asks

Endnotes

Preface

1 Peter Williams, *Jonah—Running From God* (Epsom: Day One, 2003), p. 95.

Chapter 1

1 Richard P. Belcher, *Genesis: The Beginning of God's Plan of Salvation* (Fearn, Ross-shire: Christian Focus, 2012), p. 79.

2 Richard D. Phillips, *Hebrews* (Phillipsburg, NJ: P&R Publishing, 2006), p. 403.

3 James Montgomery Boice, *Genesis* (Grand Rapids, MI: Baker, 2006), Vol. 1, p. 252.

4 David Gooding, *The Riches of Divine Wisdom: The New Testament's Use of the Old Testament* (Coleraine, NI: Myrtlefield House, 2013), p. 196.

5 Steven Smith, *Exalting Jesus in Jeremiah and Lamentations* (Nashville, TN: Holman, 2019), p. 30.

6 Christopher Idle © Author and Jubilate Hymns.

Chapter 2

1 Christopher J.H. Wright, *How to Preach and Teach the Old Testament for All Its Worth* (Grand Rapids, MI: Zondervan, 2016), p. 58.

2 God asks the same question of the prophet Jeremiah: 'Behold, I am the LORD, the God of all flesh. Is anything to hard for me?' (Jer. 32:27). Literally, the question is, 'Is anything too wonderful for the Lord?' See Derek Kidner, *Psalms* (Downers Grove, IL: Inter-Varsity Press, 2008), p. 105.

3 Quoted in James Montgomery Boice, *Genesis: An Expositional Commentary* (Grand Rapids, MI: Baker, 2006), Vol. 2, p. 606.

4 Donald Grey Barnhouse, *Genesis: A Devotional Exposition* (Grand Rapids, MI: Zondervan, 1970), p. 185.

5 Keith Getty and Stuart Townend, 'From the breaking of the dawn' © 2005 Thankyou Music.

Chapter 3

1 Alec Motyer, *The Message of Exodus* (Nottingham: Inter-Varsity Press, 2005), p. 69.

2 Motyer, *The Message of Exodus*, pp. 69–70.

3 Philip Graham Ryken, *Exodus: Saved for God's Glory* (Wheaton, IL: Crossway, 2005), p. 114.

4 A.W. Pink, *Gleanings in Exodus* (Chicago: Moody, 1981), p. 38.

5 Alec Motyer, *The Message of Exodus*, p. 81.

6 Helen H. Lemmel, 'O soul, are you weary and troubled?' (1922).

7 Adapted from Alec Motyer, *The Message of Exodus*, p. 81.

8 Joseph M. Scriven, 'What a friend we have in Jesus' (1855).

Chapter 4

1 The website of the United Methodist Church at www.umcdiscipleship. org/resources/history-of-hymns accessed 28 September 2019.

2 For a discussion of these two renderings of verse 3, see Dale Ralph Davis, *1 Kings: The Wisdom and the Folly* (Fearn, Ross-shire: Christian Focus, 2002), pp. 257–65.

3 Philip Graham Ryken, *1 Kings* (Phillipsburg, NJ: P&R Publishing, 2011), p. 526.

4 Ibid. p. 260.

5 Elizabeth C. Clephane, 'Beneath the cross of Jesus' (1868).

Chapter 5

1 David Schneider on Twitter @davidschneider 8 July, 2016, accessed 29 September 2019.

2 John Mackay, *Isaiah* (Darlington: Evangelical Press, 2008), Vol. 1, p. 163.

3 Thomas Binney, 'Eternal Light! Eternal Light!' (1826).

4 'A Prophet Commissioned'—sermon preached at All Souls Church, Langham Place, London, 24 July 2016.

5 John Murray, *Redemption: Accomplished and Applied* (Grand Rapids, MI: William Eerdmans, 1955).

6 David Jackman, in a sermon preached at St Helen's, Bishopsgate, London, 23 January 2011.

7 John Ellerton, 'The day Thou gavest, Lord, is ended' (1870).

Chapter 6

1 Verses 3–5 are quoted in part or in full in Matthew 3:3; Mark 1:3, Luke 3:4-6 and John 1:23. Verses 6–8 are quoted in 1 Peter 1:24–25.

2 William Philip, in a sermon on Isaiah 40 preached at Holyrood Abbey Church, Edinburgh, 11 March 1979.

3 D. Martyn Lloyd-Jones, *The All-Sufficient God: Sermons on Isaiah 40* (Edinburgh: Banner of Truth, 2005), p. 83.

4 Henry Francis Lyte, 'Praise, my soul, the King of heaven' (1834).

5 Quoted in J.I. Packer, *Knowing God* (London: Hodder & Stoughton, 2013), p. 98.

6 Ibid.

7 Edward J. Young, *The Book of Isaiah* (Grand Rapids, MI: William B. Eerdmans, 1972), Vol. 3, p. 61.

Chapter 7

1 William Hendriksen, *Exposition of the Gospel According to Matthew* (Grand Rapids, MI: Baker Academic, 1973), p. 429.

2 Richard D. Phillips, *2 Samuel* (Phillipsburg, NJ: P&R Publishing, 2018), p. 148.

3 Horatius Bonar, 'I heard the voice of Jesus say' (1846).

Chapter 8

1 Steven Smith, *Exalting Jesus in Jeremiah and Lamentations* (Nashville, TN: Holman, 2019), p. 81.

2 Quoted in Philip Graham Ryken, *Jeremiah and Lamentations* (Wheaton, IL: Crossway, 2001), p. 220.

3 This was mistranslated by the King James Version as the 'swellings of Jordan' suggesting a river in flood. But God is referring rather to the thick undergrowth that grows along the bank of the Jordan—a haunt of lions (see Jeremiah 49:19; 50:44)—making it a difficult and dangerous place to walk. Google a picture of the Jordan river and you'll see what is meant.

Chapter 9

1 Charles W. Colson, *Who Speaks for God? Confronting the World with Real Christianity* (London: Hodder & Stoughton, 1985), p. 20.

2 Elsewhere in the Bible, Shallum is called Jehoahaz (2 Kings 10:35) and Coniah is called Jehoiachin (2 Kings 24:6).

3 Christopher J.H. Wright, *The Message of Jeremiah* (Nottingham: Inter-Varsity Press, 2014), p. 251.

4 These three points were gleaned from a sermon by David Jackman at the Evangelical Ministry Assembly, 1996.

5 Philip Graham Ryken, *Jeremiah and Lamentations* (Wheaton, IL: Crossway, 2001), p. 355.

6 Charles W. Colson, *Who Speaks for God?*, p. 22.

7 Keith Getty and Stuart Townend © 2005 Thankyou Music.

Chapter 10

1 I am grateful to Christopher J.H. Wright for suggesting the basis of this outline in, *The Message of Ezekiel* (Nottingham: Inter-Varsity Press, 2001), pp. 304–308.

2 Derek Thomas, *Ezekiel: God Strengthens* (Welwyn Garden City: EP Books, 2016), p. 290.

3 Cain in Genesis 4:9; Elijah in 1 Kings 19:10; Isaiah in Isaiah 6:8.

4 Alexander Maclaren, *The Books of Ezekiel, Daniel and the Minor Prophets* (London: Hodder and Stoughton, 1908), p. 28.

5 Ibid.

6   Edward Cooper, 'Father of heaven, whose love profound' (1805).

Chapter 11

1   Pew Research Center poll, 'Why Americans Go (and Don't Go) to Religious Services', published August 1, 2018.

2   John L. Mackay, *Haggai, Zechariah and Malachi* (Fearn, Ross-shire: Christian Focus, 2003), p. 175.

3   Richard D. Phillips, *Zechariah* (Phillipsburg, NJ: P&R Publishing, 2007), p. 159.

4   Martyn Lloyd-Jones, *Sanctified Through the Truth* (Wheaton, IL: Crossway, 1989), p. 85.

5   Collect for the Seventh Sunday after Trinity, *Book of Common Prayer* (1662).

Chapter 12

1   See Tony Bennett, *But God … The gospel in two words* (Leominster: Day One, 2018), Vol. 2, p. 111.

2   Quoted in Richard D. Phillips (Phillipsburg, NJ: P&R Publishing, 2018), p. 228.

3   William Hendriksen, *Matthew* (Grand Rapids, MI: Baker Academic, 1973), p. 357.

4   G.B. Caird, *Saint Luke* (London: Penguin Books, 1963), p. 106.

5   David Jackman, in a sermon preached on 9 December 2012 at St Helen's, Bishopsgate, London.

6   John Ellerton, 'Shine now upon us, Lord' (1881).

Chapter 13

1   Michael J. Wilkins, *The NIV Application Commentary: Matthew* (Grand Rapids, MI: Zondervan, 2004), p. 339.

2   Matthew will later give us another account of Jesus' healing two blind men near Jericho—see Matt. 20:29–34. This miracle is included by both Mark 10:46–52 and Luke 18:35–43.

3 See 2 Samuel 7:12–16.

4 Daniel Doriani, *Matthew* (Phillipsburg, NJ: P&R Publishing, 2008), Vol. 1, p. 403.

5 Ibid.

6 See, for example, John 2:11; 2:23; 3:2; 4:54; 6:2; 6:14; 6:26.

7 See, for example, Isaiah 35:5–6 as well as Exodus 4:11; Psalm 146:7–8; Isaiah 29:18 and Isaiah 42:7.

8 Charlotte Elliott, 'Just as I am—without one plea' (1834 and 1836).

Chapter 14

1 Charles Wesley, 'Hark! the herald angels sing' (1739).

2 The Nicene Creed.

3 George W. Doane, 'Thou art the way—to Thee alone' (1824).

4 C.S. Lewis, *Mere Christianity,* quoted in Jonathan Gould, *What Christians Believe* (Fearn, Ross-shire: Christian Focus, 2012), pp. 79–80.

Chapter 15

1 Dietrich Bonhoeffer, *The Cost of Discipleship* (New York: Collier, 1953), p. 99.

2 Richard D. Phillips, *John* (Phillipsburg, NJ: P&R Publishing, 2014), Vol. 1, p. 114.

3 Daniel M. Doriani, *Matthew* (Phillipsburg, NJ: P&R Publishing, 2008), Vol. 2, p. 99.

4 Michael J. Wilkins, *The NIV Application Commentary: Matthew* (Grand Rapids, MI: Zondervan, 2004), p. 572.

5 J.C. Ryle, *Matthew: Expository Thoughts on the Gospels* (Edinburgh: The Banner of Truth Trust, 2012), p. 163.

6 Marion E. Wade, *The Lord Is My Counsel: A Businessman's Personal Experience with the Bible* (Englewood Cliffs, NJ: Prentice-Hall, 1966), p. 43.

7 Lucy Ann Bennett, 'O teach me what it meaneth' (1908).

Chapter 16

1   R. Kent Hughes, *Luke* (Wheaton, IL: Crossway, 2015), p. 180.

2   David Gooding, *According to Luke: The Third Gospel's Ordered Historical Narrative* (Coleraine: Myrtlefield Trust, 1987), p. 107.

3   See, for example, Romans 6:4; Ephesians 5:2, 8, 15.

4   Charles Wesley, 'O for a thousand tongues to sing' (1739).

5   Ibid.

Chapter 17

1   Charles Colson, In Memoriam video published on YouTube by Zondervan, 2012. Accessed 1 February 2020.

Chapter 18

1   I am grateful to David Turner for this story—from his sermon, 'The dinner gate-crashed by a sinner', preached at All Souls Church, Langham Place, London, 13 September 2009.

2   Ibid. p. 346.

3   Augustus M. Toplady, 'Rock of ages, cleft for me' (1775).

4   Charlotte Elliott, 'Just as I am without one plea' (1834).

5   John Pantry, 'Wonderful grace' © Harper Collins (1986).

Chapter 19

1   Roy Hattersley, *A Brand from the Burning: The Life of John Wesley* (London: Little, Brown, 2002), p. 104.

2   Johann Andreas Rothe, 'Now I have found the ground wherein' (1725), translated by John Wesley (1740).

Chapter 20

1   *Manchester Evening News*, 5 April 2018. Accessed online 5 February 2020.

2 Deuteronomy 6:4–5; Leviticus 19:18.

3 G.B. Caird, *Saint Luke* (London: Penguin Books, 1963), p. 148.

4 Alexander Maclaren, *The Gospel of Luke*, p. 144.

5 William M. Cwirla, 'What Must I Do? A Question of the Law', *Modern Reformation*, November/December 2002, p. 6, quoted in Philip Graham Ryken, Luke (Phillipsburg, NJ: P&R Publishing, 2009), Vol. 1, p. 548.

6 Timothy Dudley-Smith, 'O God, whose all-sustaining hand' (© Author, Oxford University Press).

Chapter 21

1 For example, John 9:1–3 when Jesus was asked if a man born blind was the victim of God's judgement on his own or on his parent's sin, and Jesus replied that neither was correct. The book of Job offers another cautionary example when Job's friends took their orthodox and biblical theology but drew from it a completely erroneous application with unfortunate and pastorally insensitive consequences.

2 Philip Graham Ryken, *Luke* (Phillipsburg, NJ: P&R Publishing, 2009), Vol. 2, p. 6.

3 Richard D. Phillips, *What Happens After Death?* (Phillipsburg, NJ: P&R Publishing, 2011), p. 10.

4 Samuel Rodigast, 'Whate'er my God ordains is right' (1675).

Chapter 22

1 Richard D. Phillips, *Mighty to Save: Discovering God's Grace in the Miracles of Jesus* (Phillipsburg, NJ: P&R Publishing, 2001), p. 190.

2 Philip Graham Ryken.

3 Richard Phillips, *Mighty to Save,* p. 201.

4 Alexander Maclaren, *Expositions of Holy Scripture* (Grand Rapids, MI: Eerdmans, 1959), Vol. 6, p. 104.

5 Samuel Davies, 'Great God of wonders! all Thy ways'.

Chapter 23

1   R.C. Sproul, *John: St Andrew's Expositional Commentary* (Orlando, FL: Reformation Trust, 2009), p. 40.

2   Bessie P. Head, 'O Breath of life' (c. 1914).

Chapter 24

1   J.C. Ryle, John: Expository Thoughts on the Gospels (Edinburgh: The Banner of Truth Trust, 2012), Vol. 1, p. 277.

2   Boice, *John*, p. 531.

3   Ibid. p. 536.

4   A.W. Pink, *Exposition of the Gospel of John* (Grand Rapids, MI: Zondervan, 1975), p. 361.

5   Horatius Bonar, 'Thy works, not mine, O Christ' (1857).

Chapter 25

1   James Montgomery Boice, *John: An Expositional Commentary* (Grand Rapids, MI: Baker Books, 1985), Vol. 3, p. 724.

2   See also Tony Bennett, *But Now: the gospel perspective* (Leominster: Day One, 2019), chapter 15.

3   Based on Richard D. Phillips, *John* (Phillipsburg, NJ: P&R Publishing, 2014), Vol. 1, p. 162.

4   Carson, *The Gospel According to John*, p. 376.

5   The ESV in John 9:7 states that the man 'went and washed and came back seeing', but the word 'back' is not in the Greek. The KJV is closer to the original with 'and came seeing'.

6   J.C. Ryle, *John: Expository Thoughts on the Gospel* (Edinburgh: Banner of Truth Trust, 2012), Vol. 2, p. 123.

7   John Newton, 'Approach, my soul, the mercy-seat' (1779).

Chapter 26

1   By using the term 'fallen asleep', Jesus is not using a euphemism,

he's making a theological point about the resurrection of believers which he develops in verses 25-26.

2 A.W. Pink, *Exposition of the Gospel of John* (Grand Rapids, MI: Zondervan, 1975), p. 591.

3 D.A. Carson, *The Gospel According to John* (Leicester: Apollos, 1991), p. 412.

4 Pink, *Exposition of the Gospel of John*, p. 594.

5 Benjamin B. Warfield, *The Saviour of the World* (Edinburgh: Banner of Truth, 1991), p. 47.

6 Margaret Clarkson, 'In resurrection bodies' © Hope Publishing (1987).

Chapter 27

1 Christian F. Gellert, 'Jesus lives and so shall I' (1757).

2 D.A. Carson, *The Gospel According to John* (Leicester: Apollos, 1991), p. 491.

3 Carson suggests that a more accurate rendering of the first part of verse 7 would be: 'If you know me, you will know my Father also.' See ESV footnote.

4 A.W. Pink, *Exposition of the Gospel of John* (Grand Rapids, MI: Zondervan, 1975), p. 766.

Chapter 28

1 William Hendriksen, *Exposition of the Gospel According to Matthew* (Grand Rapids, MI: Baker Books, 1973), p. 971.

2 See, for example, Isaiah 13:10–11; Joel 2:30–31; Amos 8:9–10; Matthew 24:29–30.

3 John White, *Daring to Draw Near: People in Prayer* (Downers Grove, IL: InterVarsity Press, 1977), p. 153, quoted in Knox Chamblin, Matthew (Fearn, Ross-shire: Christian Focus, 2010), Vol. 2, p. 1412–13.

4 Richard D. Phillips, *John* (Phillipsburg, NJ: P&R Publishing, 2014), Vol. 1, p. 426.

5 Elizabeth Cecilia Clephane, 'Beneath the cross of Jesus' (c. 1868).

6   Horatio G. Spafford, 'When peace like a river' (1873).

Chapter 29

1   Hugh Palmer, in a sermon preached at All Soul's Church, Langham Place, London, 'Hearts Burning Within Us', 5 April 2015.

2   Norval Geldenhuys, *The Gospel of Luke* (Grand Rapids, MI: Eerdmans, 1977), p. 633.

3   Quoted in Philip Graham Ryken, *Luke* (Phillipsburg, NJ: P&R Publishing, 2009), Vol. 2, p. 648.

4   Ryken, Luke, p. 649.

5   Iain M. Duguid, *Is Jesus in the Old Testament?* (Phillipsburg, NJ: P&R Publishing, 2013), p. 12. Also, Christopher J.H. Wright, *How to Preach and Teach the Old Testament for All Its Worth* (Grand Rapids, MI: Zondervan, 2016).

6   Notice that both David and Abraham appear in Luke's genealogy of Jesus (see Luke 3:31, 34). Matthew goes one better by declaring, in his very first verse: 'The book of the genealogy of Jesus Christ, the son of David, the son of Abraham' (Matt. 1:1).

7   Bernard Barton, 'Lamp of our feet, whereby we trace' (1836).

Chapter 30

1   David Turner in a sermon, 'The Beach Breakfast', preached at All Souls Church, Langham Place, London, 27 August 2017.

2   G.R. Beasley-Murray quoted in Bruce Milne, *The Message of John* (Leicester: Inter-Varsity Press, 1993), p. 310.

3   Milne, *The Message of John*, p. 310.

4   Richard D. Phillips, *John* (Phillipsburg, NJ: P&R Publishing, 2014), pp. 696–97.

5   D.A. Carson, *The Gospel According to John* (Grand Rapids, MI: Eerdmans, 1991), p. 673.

6   Horatius Bonar (1846).

Chapter 31

1 A.W. Pink, *Exposition of the Gospel of John* (Grand Rapids, MI: Zondervan, 1975), p. 1134.

2 Much is made in some commentaries and sermons of the different words for 'love' that Jesus uses in these verses—agapao and phileo. But this overlooks the fact that elsewhere in his gospel, John uses these terms interchangeably. So, for example, when Jesus says that 'the Father loves the Son' in 3:35 and 5:20, both verbs are used. Likewise when John refers to 'the disciple whom Jesus loved' in 20:2 and 21:7. For more detail, see D.A. Carson, *The Gospel According to John* (Nottingham: Inter-Varsity Press, 1991), pp. 676-677.3.

3 C.K. Barrett, quoted in D.A. Carson, *The Gospel According to John*, p. 678.

4 The Lake of Gennesaret, the Sea of Tiberias and the Sea of Galilee come from respectively the Arabic, Aramaic and Hebrew names for the same freshwater lake.

5 Bruce Milne, *The Message of John* (Leicester: Inter-Varsity Press, 1993), p. 318.

6 William R. Featherstone, 'My Jesus, I love Thee' (1864). In this version © Praise Trust.

Epilogue

1 A.W. Pink, *Exposition of the Gospel of John* (Grand Rapids, MI: Zondervan, 1975), p. 597.

2 Philip Graham Ryken, *Jeremiah and Lamentations* (Wheaton, IL: Crossway, 2001), p. 221.

3 William Cowper (c. 1765).